Pastor Jim Cymbala is known as a man who listens to God and faithfully teaches his Word. In his book *Fan the Flame,* he has a powerful message for all who struggle in their ministry. If you are a church leader and feel the depths of discouragement and defeat because of the challenges you face among God's people, this book is for you. Throughout these pages, Pastor Cymbala speaks as a wise and godly mentor, confronting the pain of fruitlessness and rejection, teaching essential principles for successful ministry, and recounting his experiences of God's faithfulness. I pray that those tempted to abandon their calling will read this book, embrace Pastor Cymbala's wise counsel, and be strengthened to carry on in God's plan for their lives.

DR. CHARLES STANLEY, founder of In Touch Ministries
and pastor emeritus of First Baptist Atlanta

In *Fan the Flame,* Jim Cymbala confronts head-on the crisis facing pastors and leaders across America. Biblically sound and spiritually inspirational!

DR. TONY EVANS, president of the Urban Alternative
and senior pastor at Oak Cliff Bible Fellowship

Jim Cymbala has the rare gift of being able to cut through all the clutter and get to our hearts as ministers and Christian workers. This book is written to encourage and redirect those who are weary and confused amid the increasing pressures and expectations of our culture. You will be blessed to read these pages and then be sure to pass the book along to your pastor or anyone who wants to fan the flame flickering in their hearts.

ERWIN W. LUTZER, pastor emeritus of Moody Church, Chicago

We are reminded that God is sovereign and in control of it all. You will find solace, practical advice, and strength to step out of the way so God can reignite passion in you so your God-given call to kingdom service will flourish once again. Follow Jim Cymbala and the apostle Paul through the pages of this powerful book as they follow Christ and show us the way to put the guardrails of the timeless truth of Jesus Christ back into the church today.

RON BROWN, executive director/CEO of Teen Challenge of Southern California and international conference speaker for pastors and Christian leaders

FAN

THE

FLAME

FAN
THE
FLAME

LET JESUS RENEW YOUR CALLING

AND REVIVE YOUR CHURCH

JIM CYMBALA

WITH
JOHN BLATTNER

ZONDERVAN REFLECTIVE

Fan the Flame
Copyright © 2022 by Jim Cymbala

Requests for information should be addressed to:
Zondervan, 3900 *Sparks Dr. SE, Grand Rapids, Michigan 49546*

Zondervan titles may be purchased in bulk for educational, business, fundraising, or sales promotional use. For information, please email SpecialMarkets@Zondervan.com.

ISBN 978-0-310-13379-7 (international trade paper edition)
ISBN 978-0-310-13378-0 (audio)

Library of Congress Cataloging-in-Publication Data

Names: Cymbala, Jim, 1943- author. | Blattner, John, author.
Title: Fan the flame : let Jesus renew your calling and revive your church / Jim Cymbala with John Blattner.
Description: Grand Rapids : Zondervan, 2022.
Identifiers: LCCN 2022013703 (print) | LCCN 2022013704 (ebook) | ISBN 9780310133766 (hardcover) | ISBN 9780310133773 (ebook)
Subjects: LCSH: Bible. Acts, XX—Criticism, interpretation, etc. | Church—Biblical teaching. | Church renewal. | Church growth—Biblical teaching. | BISAC: RELIGION / Christian Living / Professional Growth | RELIGION / Christian Ministry / General
Classification: LCC BS2625.6.C5 C96 2022 (print) | LCC BS2625.6.C5 (ebook) | DDC 226.6/06—dc23/eng/20220627 LC record available at https://lccn.loc.gov/2022013703 LC ebook record available at https://lccn.loc.gov/2022013704

All Scripture quotations, unless otherwise indicated, are taken from The Holy Bible, New International Version®, NIV®. Copyright © 1973, 1978, 1984, 2011 by Biblica, Inc.® Used by permission of Zondervan. All rights reserved worldwide. www.Zondervan.com. The "NIV" and "New International Version" are trademarks registered in the United States Patent and Trademark Office by Biblica, Inc.®

Scripture quotations marked NKJV are taken from the New King James Version®. Copyright © 1982 by Thomas Nelson. Used by permission. All rights reserved.

Scripture quotations marked NLT are taken from the Holy Bible, New Living Translation. © 1996, 2004, 2015 by Tyndale House Foundation. Used by permission of Tyndale House Publishers, Inc., Carol Stream, Illinois 60188. All rights reserved.

Any internet addresses (websites, blogs, etc.) and telephone numbers in this book are offered as a resource. They are not intended in any way to be or imply an endorsement by Zondervan, nor does Zondervan vouch for the content of these sites and numbers for the life of this book.

Published in association with the literary agency of Ann Spangler and Company, 1415 Laurel Ave. SE, Grand Rapids, MI 49506.

Cover design: Nicole Forman
Cover photo: Maxim Tajer / Unsplash
Interior design: Denise Froehlich

Printed in the United States of America

22 23 24 25 26 27 28 29 30 31 32   /LSC/   16 15 14 13 12 11 10 9 8 7 6 5 4 3 2

*To my wife, Carol, whose musical
gifting from God and tireless labor have
helped expand the kingdom of God*

CONTENTS

CHAPTER 1

A Tale of Two Departures

*From Miletus, Paul sent to Ephesus for the
elders of the church. When they arrived, he said
to them: "You know how I lived the whole time
I was with you, from the first day I came into
the province of Asia."*

—ACTS 20:17–18

After church services on a Sunday in March 2020, my wife, Carol, and I headed for a four-day getaway to Florida. The next day, one of my associate pastors in Brooklyn called informing me that the COVID-19 pandemic had forced the closing of the schools and the courts. New Yorkers were now hunkered down in their homes. No one seemed to know much about where all this was heading. One thing was certain: our church office was closed, and all our meetings had been canceled until further notice.

In the months that followed, some severe COVID-19 spikes devastated the city where I was born and raised. Our vacation plans turned into more than a year away from the Brooklyn Tabernacle, the church Carol and I have led for more than five decades.

While stranded in Florida, we were contacted by different

denominational leaders who asked if we would meet with small groups of pastors. We made ourselves available, and for months—almost weekly—we met with pastors and their wives from various denominations, as well as other independent church leaders. I listened as they shared how they entered the ministry and talked about their present situation, their hopes, and the special pressures they now faced.

After hearing many stories and visiting some of the well-known churches in the area, I developed a deep burden in my heart for the Christian church and its leadership. I met many sincere people who wanted to see their ministries and congregations make a real difference in their communities. Their frustration and the effects of their discouragement were obvious.

After all our experiences at the Brooklyn Tabernacle, and having begun there with fewer than twenty people in the congregation, Carol and I knew something about the challenges of ministry. But attending some services locally opened my eyes to another whole set of problems. This led me to many hours of sitting before the Lord with an open Bible, that I might hear what the Holy Spirit would give me to help pastors and their churches get a fresh start.

We Christians are all on the same team. If one hurts, we should all feel it; and if one is blessed, we should all rejoice. This book is my heartfelt endeavor to bring encouragement to the body of Christ and especially to church leaders. It has no magic formula or personal vision I wish to communicate. It's just a sincere attempt to review what we're doing and why we're doing it, in light of God's Word.

What's Going On Here?

Every day, across America, people leave their churches. There are a lot of reasons why. Their circumstances change. They change jobs, they move away. They encounter personal challenges. They lose their faith. They quit because they're alienated or upset about something. Whatever the reasons, every one of these situations has a story. Here is one of them.

Matt and Sarah (not their real names) found the Lord in our church in Brooklyn. They were born again, were baptized, and started going to church, serving the Lord, studying the Bible, fellowshipping, coming to prayer meetings—a beautiful story of God's grace.

When a job opportunity for Matt became available in another state, one of their first priorities was to find a church there. They thrived in their new place of worship for several years. But around the fifth year, things started to change, in small ways at first: for example, the praise and worship became more production oriented. Instead of the simplicity of people singing to God, which is what worship is supposed to be, it felt more like a concert. The worship team was seamlessly moving through the numbers they had practiced during the week. The band had it together. But after a while, it became clear that most of the congregation didn't know the songs. About 20 percent were trying to sing along while the others watched and clapped. Instead of the congregation directing worship to God, it was being entertained. God wasn't the audience anymore; the congregation was.

The preaching changed as well. The focus was less on proclaiming the Word of God than on showcasing the plans, goals, and vision of the church. Sermons became like pep talks, with the pastor as life coach. The Sunday services were meticulously planned and slickly produced, but Matt and Sarah felt that they walked out of church on Sundays no closer to Jesus than they were when they walked in.

They tried attending a couple of the small group meetings the church offered. Most of them were more like social events where folks hung out and made small talk. There was little Bible study and no real prayer. At some, alcoholic beverages were served. This was worrisome to Matt and Sarah, since one of them had come from a background where alcohol abuse was a serious problem. The more they listened to the way the people talked— the language they used, and what they talked about—the more Matt and Sarah thought, "Wait a minute. This is the way I used to live before I found Christ. What's going on here?"

Sarah then noticed that Matt wasn't doing well. Some old patterns were creeping back into his life. Soon there were signs that he was texting and getting involved with other women. Sarah desperately needed help. But the church had none to offer. It didn't practice church membership, so there was no spiritual authority whereby a pastor, as a loving shepherd, could take a member of the flock aside and say, "We need to talk. We need to pray together." They tried a couple of other churches in the area but found them little different from the first one. Matt's spiritual health continued to deteriorate, and Sarah and their two children continued to suffer the consequences.

By the time Sarah got in touch with me, she and Matt were already divorced. To make matters worse, Matt's relationship with the children was in tatters. The last time Matt challenged his teenaged son about something, he said to the boy, "Don't you lie to me!" His son fired back, "You're telling me not to lie, after what you've done to Mom?"

I don't yet know how the story will end. Matt has walled himself off from Sarah. I recently left a message for him, telling him, "I'm here. We go way back. You're not the man I knew. I don't want to yell at you or preach at you. I just want you to know I'm available." So far, as I write these words, he hasn't gotten back to me.

I don't hold Matt and Sarah's church, or its pastor, solely

responsible for what happened. Ultimately, each of us needs to "work out [our] salvation with fear and trembling" (Phil. 2:12). But I can't help but think that Matt and Sarah might have ended up in a different place had their church offered more spiritual strengthening rather than mere Sunday entertainment.

I also think that the story of this couple is not an isolated case. A recent Gallup poll found that for the first time since they started polling in the 1930s, the number of Americans who describe themselves as affiliated with a church, synagogue, or mosque has fallen below 50 percent.[1] Actual church attendance is even lower. According to one recent survey, only about a third of Americans attended services every (or almost every) week in 2020; more than 50 percent say they attended "seldom" or "never."[2] Are these negative trends not stunning? But it's happening across the board. Leaders from almost all the major Protestant denominations and traditions give the same report: church members are leaving for one reason or another, and as a result many local assemblies are shutting down. Denominations are doing their best to plant new churches and absorb other independent churches. But the fact remains that fewer people now go to church in America than ever before.

Then there's the case of the missing millennials. In 2002 millennials made up the vast majority of the audiences of "contemporary churches." At that time, they were in their early twenties; today those same millennials would be in their forties, married, with possibly one to two kids. But where are they? Many have moved on from the contemporary churches they attended, with a new population of twentysomethings taking their place. But there's no evidence they've moved en masse to other congregations, since Christian churches are declining in attendance across the board. Statistics show us that the great majority aren't going to church at all. But why? Why would they leave the churches where they first met Christ? Perhaps they aged out of the target group those churches were built to reach. If that's true, we have a real problem. Our churches need people of *all* age groups. In fact, as believers grow in the Lord (and age-wise), they are able to serve the people of God with greater wisdom.

Discouraged, Disheartened, All but Defeated

Sadly, it's not only churchgoers who are missing from our services. I'd like to share a story about a pastor I'll call Evan. His story is typical of many pastors I've spoken with in recent years. It goes like this:

> Pastor Jim, I've been doing this for eighteen years. When I started out, I wanted to serve the Lord. I wanted to be a blessing to people. And I've tried my hardest. I've spearheaded building programs. I've painted the walls different colors because that's what some of the church growth proponents say is important to set the right atmosphere. I've spent a small fortune on new lighting. We have lots of activity. But I'm not making converts. People come, then they leave. It's like a revolving door. But changed lives? I don't see that.
>
> I've cast more than one "new vision" to my board and congregation. I got them from the experts who claim to know what works. But it's not working for me. Now I'm suffering a major decline in attendance and giving. How do I pay for my children's education? I don't want to lose my health insurance. To tell you the truth, I'm considering leaving the pastorate and selling life insurance for a living.

Evan's story is tragic. Unfortunately, it's also quite common. According to a survey conducted by the Barna Group, about

1,500 pastors leave the ministry every month.[3] Even more telling is that half the pastors polled said they would leave the ministry if they had another way to make a living. That's staggering! And the stress is taking a toll on pastors' families. In fact, over 80 percent of clergy spouses want their spouse to leave the ministry.

These are grim statistics. Other surveys paint a less dire picture, but even if we cut the numbers in half, they're still sobering. And surveys and statistics aside, my personal experience tells me that a great many pastors are discouraged, disheartened, and all but defeated.

Does any of this sound familiar? Laboring in the vineyard for years with little spiritual fruit to show for it can be discouraging. Even if a leader has been truly called, the lack of spiritual fruit leads to hidden frustration and discouragement. There comes a day when the leader can't hide it anymore. No matter how they try to cover it up, their discouragement affects everyone around them. Perhaps most tragically, it affects their family.

For many years I've felt a special burden for men and women in ministry. I've been blessed with many invitations to speak at conferences and seminars directed to leaders. But I've also had countless opportunities to sit down with small groups of pastors—one or two or five or ten at a time, from all denominational backgrounds and theological persuasions, often with their spouses—and I've listened to their stories. I ask them how they were called into the ministry, what challenges they face, and how they think God wants to use them going forward. Many of their stories are inspirational. Many blessed churches dot the landscape.

For many other pastors, though, their tone changes as the conversations deepen. I share with them some of the difficulties and discouragements Carol and I have faced over the years. Then they share their own experiences, slowly and hesitantly at first but then, as their defenses weaken, in torrents. Defeats, frustrations, personal challenges, family strains. Often tears flow. The most common, and most crushing, are the accounts of feeling as if they have failed and let God down. They try to drum up more faith and persevere; but it's tough sledding when you're just "doing church." And too many feel like they want to quit.

Who's Leaving Whom?

The two departures I recounted in this chapter are interrelated. On the one hand, we have people leaving churches because those churches have lost their spiritual calling and power. Their services resemble a shallow religious show with little spiritual food. On the other hand, we have leaders growing discouraged and worn down. From what? Could it be from beating their heads against a wall as they build revolving-door churches where people come and go every few years? We need humility to face the possibility that we might be on the wrong path. Maybe what we're building isn't what Jesus had in mind for his church.

Here's a lesson I learned playing basketball: when you take a shot, if you don't hold the ball right, if your elbow flies out, if you don't follow through—I don't care if you're wearing $300 vintage Air Jordans—chances are the ball won't go through the hoop. The best golfers in the world, when they get in a rut, go to a swing coach. What do you suppose the swing coach says to them first? He says, "Show me how you hold the club. Show me how you position your feet when you're getting ready to swing." Why? Because those elements are foundational. These are the basics. Even if you're Tiger Woods, if your fundamentals aren't sound, you won't hit the ball where you're aiming.

We must face reality. When your team is trailing 28–3 in the first quarter, when you're seven strokes over par after the third hole, you've got to have the courage to face the scoreboard.

There's a difference between faith and fantasy. Christians are leaving the church in droves and leaders are losing heart and leaving the ministry, so something is obviously wrong, and we must be open to changing course.

Every so often we need to take a step back and ask ourselves, "Are my fundamentals right?" Better yet, we should search the Scriptures and seek the Lord about our own ministry. Are we doing things his way? That's important, since it's his church we're supposed to be building, not ours. All the technology, mood lighting, and great sound systems won't help us if we're not building according to God's plan. Listen to the inspired apostle as he talks about the responsibility of building a church:

> By the grace God has given me, I laid a foundation as a wise builder, and someone else is building on it. But each one should build with care. For no one can lay any foundation other than the one already laid, which is Jesus Christ. If anyone builds on this foundation using gold, silver, costly stones, wood, hay or straw, their work will be shown for what it is, because the Day will bring it to light. It will be revealed with fire, and the fire will test the quality of each person's work. (1 Cor. 3:10–13)

The quality of every leader's work will be tested by fire at the end of the day. How tragic would it be if we found that "wood, hay or straw"—cheap, inferior things—characterized our ministries rather than the preciousness of gold, silver, and costly stones. Imagine putting in years of work, only to find that it was all worthless when tested by God's fire. Lord, help us all!

It would be wise to consider that there may be a way of doing God's work, with God's help, for God's glory, that is better than any of the formulas that have enticed us away from Jesus's vision

9

for *his church*. Formulas that only make for less fruit, more discouragement, more frustration, and—worst of all—less glory to God. Jesus said, "This is to my Father's glory, that you bear much fruit" (John 15:8).

God is waiting on many of us, today's church leaders, to pull away from our busy schedules to receive a fresh word and fresh direction from him. How could he, who has given us his only Son, fail to equip and energize us anew for the work he has called us to do? Does our Father delight in frustrating us with promises he will fail to keep? Never! He works for those who wait for him (Isa. 64:4), and his power released among us can accomplish more in one month than an entire year of human activity. We too often forget that "unless the LORD builds the house, the builders labor in vain" (Ps. 127:1).

Beware of Detours

From my conversations with pastors, I have noticed some common "detours" that lead ministers and churches off track.

Tradition

History can be instructive. But it can also be stifling because God has worked in different ways at different times. Church history and testimonies from the past may hinder our ability to follow fresh direction from the Holy Spirit.

Many leaders are stuck trying to replicate what they saw growing up in church, whether it produced spiritual fruit or not. And this nostalgia keeps them from being open to change and growth. They rarely receive fresh revelation of truth from God's Word. They are averse to any change from what they grew up around.

But we forget that the men and women who made a huge

difference for God in the past were not afraid to step out in faith in new ways. They were willing to be led by God, and as a result they turned their world upside down.

Consider the famous missionary to China, Hudson Taylor. When he refused to follow established tradition but rather chose to adopt Chinese dress and culture, he was roundly criticized. In the end, he was mightily used by God and pioneered a new approach to mission work. In a similar way, we too need to be brave in following God.

Latest Trends

Following the latest trends is the flip side of getting stuck trying to relive the past, and it is equally problematic. I'll share an example that highlights just how ridiculous—and how pernicious—it can be to follow after the latest trends in ministry.

I had been pastoring for about eight or nine years when an older pastor from another part of the city visited me. He was immersed in the leading church-growth philosophies of the time. He said, "You know, Jim, your church is an anomaly to me. I can't figure it out." I asked him what he meant. What was the "anomaly" that puzzled him? "Look at the people in your church, in your wife's choir," he said. "There's Black, West Indian, Latino, Caucasian, Asian. It's a diverse mix of people. The problem is that principle number four of the church-growth program I'm following says that churches grow faster when they are homogeneous—all from the same culture and ethnicity." I responded, "Brother, with all due respect, everyone knows what that's a code word for." That brought the conversation to a halt.

Now, I'm not denying his point. Maybe birds of a feather do flock together. That's always been true in a carnal sense. But that's not what the gospel is about. The Jews and the gentiles hated each other two thousand years ago, but the gospel broke down that wall. When they came together as the family of God, despite their differences, it was a sign of the power of the gospel. Racial and ethnic differences dissolve when God's love fills our lives.

The church-growth industry offers many options that leaders throughout the country choose from as they reach for what the world calls "success." Take, for example, marketing and social media in a digital age. These can be helpful, but they are only communication tools. In and of themselves, they can never build a spiritual church. The church is built by the pure gospel of Christ and the Spirit working among its members.

Politics

The political detour can be subtle. Without question, we are called to be a light to the world, and undoubtedly some of the church's finest hours have featured humble, dedicated Christian soldiers serving the poor, raising up the downtrodden, and working for justice. But the Bible declares that only Jesus can change the human heart, and that is what the gospel is all about. Institutional and governmental changes alone will never produce love and unity among people. The danger of politics is that we become seduced by the very structures and political forces we feel we must change.

Christian leaders sometimes form coalitions with high-ranking politicians, and by doing so, they can easily drift away from preaching the gospel. Cynical politicians value those leaders not because of an interest in Christ but because they feel that ministers will deliver the "evangelical vote" in some way or another. The tragedy is that whole segments of the church then become identified with a political party. Brothers and sisters, this is never good. When the church is identified with a political party, we lose our ability to get a hearing for the gospel because of the acrimony inherent in politics. Not only do we fail to change these political institutions, but they end up injecting us with the intolerance and venom that have characterized politics from the founding of our nation. The church thus becomes entangled with the affairs of this world, even to the point of fighting against or alongside folks who don't know the Lord. This damages our witness for Christ and hinders our work for the kingdom. The apostle Paul said, "What business is it of mine to judge those outside the church? Are you not to judge those inside?" (1 Cor. 5:12).

I recently received a heartbreaking call from a believer who lives in the suburbs of New York City. The person doesn't attend our church, but they watch our online devotionals where we go through books of the Bible. They expressed grief that the church they attend has gotten involved in politics and has moved away from the Bible. The sermons they hear seem to be more about "God and country" than Jesus and saving souls. They shared with me, "The time is too late for that. We have to preach Jesus!"

There is no record of the early apostles trying to improve the Roman Empire or any province within it. God is not interested in building up or promoting a specific country. He's intent on building his church. Jesus declared that only his followers are the salt of the earth and the light of the world. Democrats or liberals or progressives aren't the salt. Republicans or conservatives or libertarians aren't the light. *Christians* are. Our orders are not to curry favor with kings or presidents but to carry the message of Christ to everyone.

Believers around the world *should* be patriotic, but not in the way that phrase is generally understood. Patriotism may seem admirable, but Christians aren't citizens of America, Korea, Ghana, or Argentina first. Our nationality is not our home country if we believe in God's Word: "You are a chosen people, a royal priesthood, a *holy nation*, God's special possession, that you may declare the praises of him who called you out of darkness into his wonderful light. Once you were not a people, but now you are the people of God; once you had not received mercy, but now you have received mercy" (1 Peter 2:9–10, italics here and in Scripture quotes throughout the book were added by the author for emphasis).

Peter reminds us that we make up God's "holy nation," while Paul tells us that "our citizenship is in heaven" (Phil. 3:20). All nations have unfortunate histories riddled with deceit, imperialism of one kind or another, racism, and other problems. But our holy nation has a king over it named Jesus! Although his people of every race and ethnicity are scattered over the whole earth, we alone make up the one *holy nation* God is building, the nation he cherishes.

Culture

Sometimes, to make church "accessible" and "relevant" to the people around us, we try to incorporate elements of the secular culture that make them feel welcome. Here again, it is all too easy to be seduced by carnal thinking and turn our backs on God's way of doing things.

Not long ago, when our own services were shut down because of the pandemic, my family and I attended a well-known church. It was, to put it bluntly, an embarrassment. It felt more like a late-night talk show than a worship service. The pulpit was filled that morning by a popular conference speaker, and the message included off-color jokes and raunchy anecdotes. Even my eleven-year-old grandson realized it was not appropriate. His mother, my daughter, seethed throughout the service. But all around us people were laughing. As the meeting ended, the pastor tried pathetically to put a spiritual spin on it all. A few people came forward to be prayed for while the sound system blasted a secular pop song as the audience quickly exited. Not exactly the best atmosphere for drawing near to God!

I regularly encounter similar—if less extreme—problems when I visit other churches. It's as if the pastors have stopped seeking Christ for what he wants his church to be and instead have started asking people what *they* want it to be. It's consumer religion—giving people what they want instead of what God wants to give them. If you asked the leader, "Do you really think this is conducive to spiritual growth and is pleasing to God?" the answer would likely be, "Oh, you're antiquated. That's old-school thinking." But I'm not "old school," and I don't want to be "new school." And God isn't old school or new school either. God is eternal truth, and the Lord Jesus Christ is "the same yesterday and today and forever" (Heb. 13:8).

Every believer in Jesus who loves God's Word should be troubled by those who want to redefine the essence of Christ's church in the quest to "stay relevant" and appeal to their "hip" target group. The Lord has clearly spoken concerning the nature of the body of Christ. People gathering in a building to be entertained once a week does not make a Christian church. Rather, the church is a supernatural, spiritual organism created through the gospel and the power of God as a dwelling place for the Holy Spirit. To redefine the Christian church is a terrible thing in God's sight.

Our Sacred Calling

When I talk with ministers who are hurting, discouraged, and ready to quit, I often say, "Look, I don't know you well. But isn't it true that there was a moment in the past when, alone with God, you received his call on your life? And you surrendered to him. You said, 'Lord, here I am. I will serve you.' In that moment you had no doubt that God had spoken to your heart. What you need to do now is to stop and ask yourself, 'Is this really what God called me to do?' Because the first step out of your frustration and confusion is to go back to that moment and reconsecrate yourself to that sacred, high calling, no matter what may follow."

Contemplating changing course midstream can be overwhelming for any pastor. But God will be faithful. He has given us the Spirit of grace to lead us, the throne of grace to run to in our time of need, and the word of grace to share with people needing Christ.

As we fulfill the sacred calling of the Lord on our lives, we have the encouraging words of the apostle Paul: "My dear brothers and sisters, stand firm. Let nothing move you. Always give yourselves fully to the work of the Lord, because you know that your labor in the Lord is not in vain" (1 Cor. 15:58).

Notice that these words were not written to the *leaders* in the Corinth church but to the entire congregation, who Paul assumed would be busy doing the work of the Lord.

Whether we're leaders or the people in the pew, at the end of our lives, we all want to hear the Lord say, "Well done, good and faithful servant! . . . Come and share your master's happiness!" (Matt. 25:23).

The Model Pastor

God has held up Paul before us as a model minister of the gospel, regardless of the days and times in which we live.

None of the original twelve apostles had their lives put on display in the New Testament writings quite like the apostle Paul. We read about Paul's dramatic conversion—from a persecutor of the church to a follower of Christ—and then how God used him to build the early church with almost no resources: no money, no buildings, not even a written gospel. There was no New Testament, largely because Paul and others hadn't written it yet. In the book of Acts, when he is converted, the spotlight shifts from the church in Jerusalem to Paul. Paul in Antioch. Paul and Barnabas on the first missionary journey. Paul and Silas. Paul in Greece. Paul in Jerusalem. Paul in Rome. Why the shift in focus? It seems as if God points us to Paul as a role model for ministry. Technology changes. Cultures change. But the principles of Christian ministry never change. What was true for Paul two thousand years ago still applies to us today.

I've always been fascinated by Paul's address to the Ephesian elders, recorded in Acts 20. They didn't do selfies in those days. But I think this message gives us a snapshot of how Paul approached ministry and what he thought was important.

Paul had spent about three years in Ephesus at the beginning of his third missionary journey. For three months, he preached daily in the synagogue. But when he encountered opposition there, he relocated to a secular meeting place called the hall of Tyrannus, where he taught and debated daily for two years "so that all the Jews and Greeks who lived in the province of Asia heard the word of the Lord" (Acts 19:10). From there his journey took him to Greece. And then it was on to Jerusalem. But first he stopped off in Miletus, from where he "sent to Ephesus for the elders of the church" (Acts 20:17) for what amounted to a farewell address.

Paul knew the churches in and around Ephesus because he had helped build them. And he knew the elders of the churches in Ephesus, whom he had last seen little more than a year before. He knew their level of spiritual maturity, their strengths and weaknesses, and the challenges they faced.

And he knew something else. The Holy Spirit had revealed to Paul that this was going to be the last time he would ever speak to them. He told them so: "Now I know that none of you among whom I have gone about preaching the kingdom will ever see me again" (Acts 20:25). Think of the deep emotions Paul must have had as he opened his heart. Imagine you are about to speak to your own children for the last time. What words would you choose? This would be no time for a matter-of-fact conversation. A sermon with three points and a conclusion would be the last thing on your mind. Your words would come straight from your heart, from the depths of your soul. This would be the time to say everything you wouldn't want to leave unsaid when you die. Paul knew this was his last opportunity to instruct, admonish, and encourage these elders about how to care for the church of Christ, still in its infancy, that was under their care.

Do As You Have Seen Me Do

So what were his first words?

"You know how I lived the whole time I was with you, from the first day I came into the province of Asia" (Acts 20:18). Notice that Paul didn't say, "Do you remember how dynamic my preaching was? Amazing, right?" He didn't even remind them of healings or other miracles that occurred, or how the church attendance and offerings had increased. Paul started by pointing to the way he had lived among them and the example he had set by his behavior. He implied that they should follow in his footsteps, even as he followed his Lord. He made himself the model for how those leaders should live and minister.

This is a great reminder that how we live and interact with our congregations can either strengthen or weaken our spiritual authority. Our actions speak louder than our sermons. A remote, exclusive lifestyle lived apart from the flock will make it harder for them to believe we love them and understand their spiritual challenges. But there are risks when we interact with them as well. I know of instances where one harsh response or an off-color joke severely damaged a leader's credibility. We need the wisdom of Solomon to help us live among the people we serve without losing our spiritual authority.

I will use Paul's speech in Acts 20 as a template for this book. We'll try to understand what Paul did in Ephesus and how we can learn from his example. As we go over parts of Paul's talk to the Ephesian elders, let's not assume we understand even the most familiar phrases, for God might have new lessons for us in the very places we skip over so easily. I hope you will read this book with the same carefulness and prayerfulness that I have tried to bring to the writing of it. Let's always keep in mind that what Paul faced was a more daunting task than what we face today.

When Paul visited Ephesus, it was a large city in the Roman Empire, in today's Turkey. Although it was situated some miles from the coast, a broad channel led to its famous harbor. In the city was the opulent Temple of Artemis, one of the seven wonders of the ancient world. There was also its enormous theater, open to the sky, which held twenty-five thousand spectators. Ephesus was the capital of Proconsular Asia and a seat of government. Paul's first visit was brief, but his second stay resulted in three years of fruitful ministry. As best we can tell, Paul resided almost exclusively in the city, while his converts spread to areas beyond, planting churches as they went.

What Paul encountered in Ephesus was a wealthy cosmopolitan city filled with superstition (the Roman army often made military decisions by trying to read the meaning of chicken droppings), idolatry (the Roman pantheon of gods included hundreds of deities), and other pagan vices common to the Roman Empire (mistresses often lived in the same house with the wife and children). There was no Judeo-Christian influence present in the culture. With no large (if any) Christian community, Paul faced the daunting task of teaching the foreign message of a Jewish carpenter who died in Jerusalem. Opposition to his work developed quickly, yet Paul stayed the course and saw an amazing response to the gospel through the power of the Holy Spirit.

Against all odds, God used Paul to ignite a mighty spiritual revival in that pagan city. So why can't the Lord, in the same way, use us to light a fire wherever he has placed us? Why can't we too see spiritual breakthroughs so the world around us might experience the warmth of God's love? My prayer is that the lessons Paul taught will help us become the leaders we've always wanted to be and, even more importantly, the leaders we know *God* wants us to be.

CHAPTER 2

THE HEART OF MINISTRY

I served the Lord with great
humility and with tears.

—ACTS 20:19

Let's return to the scene I introduced at the end of the previous chapter. Paul is saying farewell to the elders of Ephesus, and he reminds them of his ministry among them. In another of his letters, Paul identified himself as "Paul, a servant of Christ Jesus" (Rom. 1:1). Now, there are two Greek words for our English word *servant*. One of them refers to someone who voluntarily accepts employment in the service of someone else. Think, for example, of the butlers and maids hired to work in Buckingham Palace. But the Greek word used here, *doulos*, is sometimes translated as "bondservant." A bondservant is a slave, a person whose entire life is lived at the mercy and whim of another person. What does a slave do? They obey their master. Period. There are no arguments. No personal agendas or priorities. A bondservant has no rights. When Paul told the elders that during the three years he spent in Ephesus, he *served* the Lord (Acts 20:19), he was telling them that's what it looks like to be a slave of Jesus Christ.

Slavery is typically a miserable existence, unless, of course, your master is Jesus Christ—the one who died for you, loves you, and cares about everything in your life. Then it's the most glorious life in the world.

The church God is building is not a democracy. It's not a government of the people, by the people, for the people. We have that form of government here on earth. But the kingdom of heaven is just that: a kingdom, an absolute monarchy. By calling himself a bondservant Paul was saying, "I belong to Christ. I am under orders. I want to fulfill his will for my life. I'm not in it for fame or fortune. It's not people I want to please. My only goal in life is to hear him say, 'Well done, good and faithful servant!'"

Leadership Is Crucial

While being a minister is challenging, it's also a tremendous privilege. We should always remember that whatever is happening today in the White House, in Congress, or on Wall Street pales in comparison to the important work God has given us. Our work, unlike all other forms of service and leadership, has eternal consequences. You've probably seen the painting of Jesus standing next to the United Nations building, knocking to get in. But Christ's great aim is not to get into the United Nations. What he wants most of all is to be more welcome in our churches. And you and I are perfectly situated to help that come about. All that's necessary is for us to surrender to his plan for our ministries and congregations.

We should bear in mind that the spiritual condition of any church greatly depends on the leadership it gets from its pastors. It's difficult for a congregation to rise higher in spiritual growth and maturity than its shepherd. If the pastor is lukewarm about the things of God and the Spirit, what hope is there for the congregation to be on fire?

Many of us have read the sermons and studied the lives of great preachers from the past. That's a wise practice, in my view. But we can never fully know the effectiveness of any pastor, then or now, except by walking among the members of their church. There will always be carnal people in any church, but if you see lukewarmness and a lack of fervor in the congregation as a whole, the pastor has somehow fallen short in their responsibility. Eloquent or carefully prepared sermons don't always produce a Spirit-filled, Christlike congregation. Martin Luther once became so angry at the carnality of his congregation in Wittenberg, Germany, that he went on strike for weeks and refused to preach!

On the other hand, Paul wrote to the church in Corinth: "Do we need, like some people, letters of recommendation to you or from you? You yourselves are our letter, written on our hearts, known and read by everyone. You show that you are a letter from Christ, the result of our ministry, written not with ink but with the Spirit of the living God, not on tablets of stone but on tablets of human hearts" (2 Cor. 3:1–3).

What a testimony! They were a "letter from Christ," the result of Paul's ministry.

We have a great privilege as ministers of the gospel, but with that privilege comes great responsibility. As James put it, "Not many of you should become teachers, my fellow believers, because you know that we who teach will be judged more strictly" (James 3:1). The longer I pastor, the more I appreciate the awesome responsibility of the ministry. Spiritual leaders are involved with matters of eternal life and eternal death. Whether we minister to wealthy professional people or the homeless, the power of Jesus is the only thing that can rescue them before it's too late. We're not heroes when we preach the gospel; we're bondservants doing what we've been commanded to do. That's why

Paul said, "When I preach the gospel, I cannot boast, since I am compelled to preach. Woe to me if I do not preach the gospel!" (1 Cor. 9:16).

We can have confidence that God would not call us and send us out to minister without making all the resources of heaven available to us. He doesn't commission us and leave us on our own. When we answer his call and go out in obedience to his command, we can trust that everything we need will be available for the asking. Many times we forget this. I certainly did when I was younger. Just working harder, trying harder, and thinking harder will not build the kingdom. Only the power and provision of God will do it.

Certainly, there will be setbacks. Sometimes we will pour our hearts into helping someone, only to see them take two steps forward and one step backward. Other times they will take one step forward and then take two, or even three, steps backward, and it will discourage us. Satan will come and tell us that it's hopeless and we should give up. In those times, we need to once again take encouragement from Paul: "My dear brothers and sisters, stand firm. Let nothing move you. Always give yourselves fully to the work of the Lord, because you know that your labor in the Lord is not in vain" (1 Cor. 15:58).

Through God's grace we've got to keep doing what we do with faithfulness, diligence, and tenacity. Every sermon, every counseling session, every funeral, every hospital visit is important. These things matter to people, and they matter to the Lord. I learned long ago that the three *p*'s of ministry are *preach, pray,* and *plod.* Sometimes just to keep on plodding is what is most needed from you. Keep moving ahead, day after day, week after week, year after year. As the popular slogan says, "Just do it." Though it may sometimes feel as if you aren't making any progress, from time to time you will get the chance to look back and rejoice in all that God has done. Face every new day as a day in which to fulfill the ministry God has given you and to realize that even the plodding you do, day after day, is never in vain.

People, Not Programs

Never forget that God uses people, not programs, to bring about his kingdom on earth. God has never sought clever methods or techniques to get his work done. But today's church is looking more and more like corporate America, reducing every activity to a method, a formula, a marketing design for our "brand." The message we hear from many quarters is, "Here's the formula. Follow these steps and you can't miss." Over the past years, new formulas have come and gone, each one promising to be *the* answer. But how can any formula be from God if it's going to be replaced a few years later? The truth is, God doesn't use formulas or methods. He uses people. He uses frail people, simple people, *sinful* people. Why? Because that's all he has!

> Brothers and sisters, think of what you were when you were called. Not many of you were wise by human standards; not many were influential; not many were of noble birth. But God chose the foolish things of the world to shame the wise; God chose the weak things of the world to shame the strong. God chose the lowly things of this world and the despised things—and the things that are not—to nullify the things that are, so that no one may boast before him. (1 Cor. 1:26–29)

Jesus picked fishermen and tax collectors to be his first disciples. He chose people who would be helpless and who would need to depend on the Holy Spirit in all things—men and women whose prayer would be, "Oh, God, help me!" Personally,

I feel the most God has ever used me is when I've been hanging by a thread.

Whatever leadership position you occupy, you are there only because you were divinely called. In his letter to the Ephesians, Paul introduced himself as "an apostle of Christ Jesus *by the will of God*" (Eph. 1:1). No Bible school, committee, or denomination can make someone a real minister of the gospel of Jesus Christ. The calling and the gifting have to come first from God.

Too often we swallow what the culture tells us is all-important to gain acceptance. For example, conventional wisdom has it that the more degrees a person earns, the better they will be in their field. But having more degrees doesn't always translate into more effective ministry. I think of a young man who came into my office a few years ago. He was a sincere fellow, educated at seminary, eager to serve the Lord.

"Pastor Jim," he said, "can I open my heart?"

"Of course," I said. "What's on your mind?"

"I'm at a crossroads. I want to be used by God. The thing is . . ." He seemed to be groping for words. "The thing is, I've got my master's degree, and now I have the opportunity to get my PhD. What do you think I should do? I'm stressed out about this decision."

I said, "Listen, brother. I don't know God's plan for your life. I really don't. But let me tell you about the world I live in and how I view it. You're sitting here in my office. If you look out the window, you'll see thousands of people walking around who need Jesus. Some are sober, some aren't. Some are straight, some are gay. Some are wealthy, while others live on the street. If they think of God at all, the last thing any of them thinks is, 'God, I'm desperate. I need help. Please send someone with a PhD to rescue me.'"

Every minister must be led by God in their educational

decisions, but without doubt the greatest need for today is simple, Spirit-equipped workers who know their Bible and are filled with his love.

Can you guess the quality God looks for most? It's not intellect or academic prowess. It's not eloquence. It's not a captivating personality. No, the quality God looks for most is *availability to him*. If we're submissive as bondservants he can use us. But if we have our own agendas, none of our talents or abilities will do much good to change the world around us. The Holy Spirit is searching for people who love God and are available to be used by him. "The eyes of the LORD range throughout the earth to strengthen those whose hearts are fully committed to him" (2 Chron. 16:9).

True Humility

Paul said, "I served the Lord with great humility" (Acts 20:19). How strange these words sound! How many of us would begin to describe our ministry by first pointing to our humility? But we need to understand what true humility is. Andrew Murray maintained that "humility is not so much a virtue along with the others, but is the root of all, because it alone takes the right attitude before God and allows Him, as God, to do all."[1]

Most of us link humility to an awareness that we are sinners. We might think of the words of Isaiah: "Woe to me! . . . I am ruined! For I am a man of unclean lips" (Isa. 6:5). There's no question that recognizing our failings helps us not to think too highly of ourselves. But humility has to be more than just a consciousness of guilt, since Jesus had no sin to feel guilty about, yet he was the humblest person to walk the earth. The apostle Paul speaks of Jesus's humility in his letter to the Philippians:

> Who, being in very nature God,
>> did not consider equality with God something
>> to be used to his own advantage;
> rather, he made himself nothing
>> by taking the very nature of a servant,
>> being made in human likeness.
> And being found in appearance as a man,
>> he humbled himself
>> by becoming obedient to death—
>>> even death on a cross! (Phil. 2:6-8)

The only way to know true humility is by looking at Jesus, who was always conscious of his total dependence on the Father. He said, "The Son can do nothing by himself" (John 5:19). This is how we too should live daily, following the example of our Lord. It should also be how we approach our ministries. When we get up to preach, we need to know we have nothing in ourselves to offer unless God first pours it into us. This sense of being an empty vessel is the heart of true humility.

But we can easily become full of ourselves and lose that childlike dependency on the Lord. Here's a sobering thought: If someone is filled with a demon, the demon can be cast out. But if we are full of ourselves, that's a different, and perhaps even more difficult, problem. I often wonder what the angels think when they look down and see us so self-assured, even though our very breath is a gift from God and can be taken from us at any moment.

The truth is, if we think we're something special apart from God, he has to empty us before he can use us. But if we recognize our need, he will fill us, and we will be fit for the Lord's use. A Puritan writer once said that the main work of God each day is to bring down the proud and lift up the humble. He does this to bring us to a place of blessing, since "God resists the proud, but gives grace [only] to the humble" (James 4:6 NKJV). No wonder Scripture instructs us to "humble yourselves, therefore, under God's mighty hand, that he may lift you up in due time" (1 Peter 5:6). Jesus illustrated this principle with a parable:

> When someone invites you to a wedding feast, do not take the place of honor, for a person more distinguished than you may have been invited. If so, the host who invited both of you will come and say to you, "Give this person your seat." Then, humiliated, you will have to take the least important place. But when you are invited, take the lowest place, so that when your host comes, he will say to you, "Friend, move up to a better place." Then you will be honored in the presence of all the other guests. For all those who exalt themselves will be humbled, and those who humble themselves will be exalted. (Luke 14:8–11)

Pride has no need of God, but humility helps us pray. When we're aware of how weak we are, that's when we throw ourselves on God's promise of divine supply and really pray. And that's when God can work in and through us. How sad that we don't more frequently avail ourselves of his provision, as the author of Hebrews suggests: "Let us then approach God's throne of grace with confidence, so that we may receive mercy and find grace to help us in our time of need" (4:16).

When we're tempted to point out how great our worship team sings or how awesome our facility looks, we must also remember that God will never share his glory with anyone else. Everything we own and all our gifting comes from him. The building that the Brooklyn Tabernacle meets in these days is nice enough. But what will I do when I stand before God? Show him my building? He dwells in heaven! My first book, *Fresh Wind, Fresh Fire*, won Christian Book of the Year. I am gratified that people liked it and found it helpful. But when Jesus comes again, will I impress him with my award? He wrote the Bible!

It's probably best, as a general rule, not to make too much of ourselves, our ministries, or our churches. "Let someone else praise you, and not your own mouth; an outsider, and not your own lips" (Prov. 27:2). Let's focus instead on Jesus and the marvelous things he has done for us. I tell new members publicly, as they join the church, "We're so happy God sent you here to join us. But please don't go around talking about our church. That could grieve God's Spirit, and then where would we be? By all means, invite people to the services. But lift up Christ, not the pastor or the church." Wouldn't it be wonderful if we all forgot about highlighting our church, denomination, or "brand" and focused instead on boasting only in the Lord?

When we're full of ourselves and wise in our own eyes, it's impossible for God to empower and use us. But when we're weak and empty, God can do great things through us as we simply take the place of a bondservant. Paul said, "I served the Lord with great humility" (Acts 20:19). Contrast that attitude with the arrogance of the world around him. Think of the grandeur of the Roman Empire, with Caesar entering victoriously into the city of Rome in a golden chariot pulled by four white horses. Then ask yourself, Where is the Roman Empire today? Yet the church of Jesus Christ, built by simple, devoted men and women, fills the earth.

The Weeping Pastor

Paul also told the Ephesian leaders, "I served the Lord . . . with *tears*" (Acts 20:19). When was the last time you heard a minister say that? It doesn't fit our image of a contemporary pastor. We think a minister is someone who preaches sermons and officiates at weddings and funerals. Many pastors see themselves as something akin to a CEO or CFO, managing a staff and a budget or overseeing a building program. How many would even think to define themselves by their tears shed for others? But Paul does just that, and he conveys the same sentiment later in his address: "Remember that for three years I never stopped warning each of you night and day with *tears*" (Acts 20:31). Clearly, Paul felt it was important for these leaders to be reminded of his tears.

One day, many years ago, the Lord awakened me to a passage in Scripture. In his first letter to the Thessalonians, Paul wrote, "Just as a nursing mother cares for her children, so we cared for you" (2:7–8). The image is that of a woman pulling down the top of her dress and tenderly bringing the baby to her breast. In reading this, I felt as though God had shown me a missing element in my own ministry. I knew Paul had preached the gospel. I knew he followed the Holy Spirit's leading. But now I saw that he also loved people with a profound tenderness and intensity. That's what helped his preaching and ministry reach deep inside his listeners. The heart, even more than the head, is the key to speaking effectively on Christ's behalf.

I also realized that when we come before Jesus at the end of our lives, we will have nothing to offer him but the people who have found him as Savior. Those are our only trophies. As Paul said to the people he ministered to, "What is our hope, our joy, or the crown in which we will glory in the presence of our Lord Jesus when he comes? Is it not you? Indeed, you are our glory and joy" (1 Thess. 2:19–20).

How many of us evaluate our ministries in these terms? On the contrary, many leaders were taught they should never get too close to the flock and should always keep their distance because that's the only way the people would respect them. But that's not the way Paul saw it: "Because we loved you so much, we were delighted to share with you not only the gospel of God but our lives as well" (1 Thess. 2:8). He once called his flock "my dear children, for whom I am again in the pains of childbirth until Christ is formed in you" (Gal. 4:19).

I'm reminded of the time I encountered a woman in the lobby of our church. I recognized her as a member, but for one reason or another I hadn't interacted with her for quite a while. The first thing I thought when I saw her was, "She looks as if she's aged fifteen years. Her hair has gotten a lot grayer." When I shook her hand, it felt hard and calloused. She said, "Pastor Cymbala, I want you to meet someone." Next to her stood a twentysomething young man. "This is my son, Reginald," she said. "He's the first one in my family to ever get a high school diploma. And now he's going to law school!" Her eyes welled up with tears. I later learned what she had gone through to make this all possible—working three jobs and foregoing a lot of life's pleasures, all for her son. She had gone through the pains of childbirth for him many years before, and she took on even more hardships later in life to raise him and help him succeed. I'll bet she shed more than a few tears for him. But do you think she was sad or resentful about it? No. When you love someone, you freely sacrifice for them, and your heart follows them wherever they go. Ministry like that never counts the cost, nor does it become a dull routine.

The apostle Paul deeply loved people. No wonder he got through to them. Love always finds a way. Let's ask God to give us his heart for people.

The Story of David

I've told this story many times, but I want to share it here in the context of pastoral ministry. I don't know whether this happens where you live, but in New York City, folks who hardly ever step inside a church will suddenly show up at our services on Christmas and

Easter. Typically, a lot of the people who come aren't Christians. I don't know where they spend their time the rest of the year, but on those two days they come out of the woodwork. On Easter a line often winds around the building for each of our services.

We prioritize sharing the gospel as the main theme of our services on those days. The music department puts together an Easter or Christmas presentation with special music and sometimes a testimony or two from people who've had inspiring conversion experiences. I close the presentation by giving the gospel message and asking people to respond by coming forward for prayer. We pray with them, get to know them a bit, and gather their information so we can follow up with them later. It's always fulfilling. It's also exhausting.

I remember one Easter in particular. We had reached the end of our third service. I'd been on my feet most of the day, so I sat on the edge of the platform, loosened my tie and collar, and let out a few deep breaths.

Then I saw him.

Standing a few feet away, in the middle aisle, was a tall Black man I'd never seen before. He looked like he might be in his fifties. He stood there staring at me, shabbily dressed and holding a filthy-looking cap in his hands. I confess, I thought, "Oh, great. The service is over, I'm tired, and now I'm going to get hit up for money by one of the street people." That scenario is common because of where our church is located. We have a protocol we follow when this sort of thing happens. We don't want to give money to someone who's going to spend it to fuel their habit. But I didn't feel like going through the whole protocol. I figured I'd give him a few bucks and that would be that.

He walked closer.

I could see missing teeth, matted hair, several days' growth of beard. There was no telling when he'd last bathed. He was five feet or so away when it hit me: the smell. Maybe the most repulsive smell I've ever smelled—a combination of feces, urine, sweat, and alcohol.

"What's your name?" I asked him.

"David."

"Where did you stay last night?"

"Empty truck."

"How come you're not in a shelter?" By now I was really fighting the odor. It was overwhelming.

"No shelter."

I learned that David didn't like the idea of staying in a shelter. So he bounced from one place to another. He later told me that once he was in an abandoned apartment sleeping on a filthy mattress that had been left there. The cigarette he had been smoking fell onto the mattress just as he was dozing off. Providentially, his brother walked in as the mattress was set ablaze.

"How long you been on the street?"

"Couple of years."

I learned later that he'd been lying in his own urine on the sidewalk next to our building. He heard the music, got up, and stood just outside a side door, listening. He heard the gospel. He was ashamed to be seen by all the people, so he waited until the service was over before coming in.

I thought, "How much should I give him?" I fished a ten-dollar bill from my money clip and started to hand it to him. But he pushed my hand away. "I don't want your money," he said. "I want this Jesus you were talking about. I'm going to die out there."

And just like that, in that moment, my heart melted. I started to cry quietly. You know who also needed Jesus at that moment? I did. I prayed within, "God, forgive me. You sent somebody I'm supposed to help, and I'm trying to send him away with a ten-dollar bill." The Lord seemed to say, "Jim, if you have any value to me, if you have any purpose in my work, it has to do with this odor. This is the smell of the world I died for."

Just then David broke down quietly as well. He wrapped his arms around me, I hugged him to myself, and we started rocking back and forth. I don't know for how long. He was crying, I was crying. And I can tell you that in that moment, the smell I had found so repugnant became like a beautiful fragrance to me.

That was the beginning of a long relationship between David and our church. He is still special to my family. I led him to Christ, and we got him into detox the next day. When he got out, we gave him a job working in our church. I had to assess how he was doing, and I wanted to be near him. He got cleaned up and had his teeth fixed. It turns out he was only thirty-two years old and quite handsome.

David spent Thanksgiving and Christmas at our house that year. For Christmas, he gave me a hankie. Just a simple white hankie. I treasured it. It was the most meaningful Christmas gift I got that year.

Time went by. David met a beautiful African girl in the church. They got married. I did the wedding. Actually, I almost *ruined* the wedding. The minute David and I walked out on the platform, I saw the bride come in and I looked at him, handsome and dressed like a model for GQ magazine, and I lost it. Bawled like a baby. I composed myself for a time. But when we came to the vows and I started to say, "Do you take this man . . ." I lost it all over again. It turns out that serving the Lord with tears includes tears of joy, not only tears of anguish.

It bears repeating what Paul said to the Thessalonians: "What is our hope, our joy, or the crown in which we will glory in the presence of our Lord Jesus when he comes? Is it not you?" (1 Thess. 2:19).

I think that in Paul's mind, some of the jewels in that crown were the tears he had shed for the people he loved so much.

CHAPTER 3

THROUGH MANY DANGERS, TOILS, AND SNARES

I served the Lord . . . in the midst of severe
testing by the plots of my Jewish opponents.
—ACTS 20:19

B angladesh is a country in South Asia that was originally part
of India. It became a province of Pakistan when India was
partitioned in 1947 and was renamed East Pakistan in 1955. In
1971 this province became the independent nation of Bangladesh.
Today its population is approximately 90 percent Muslim, with
only 0.5 percent Christian.

I visited Bangladesh once a number of years ago. A mission
organization had invited me to join them as they traveled to
Bangladesh to train and encourage local Christian pastors facing a difficult and hostile environment in that Muslim-majority
country. Before I arrived, I had been told about a local pastor
whose story was deeply disturbing. I looked forward to meeting
him, yet I was slightly uneasy, given his recent circumstances.

At the meeting, the pastors and other local church leaders followed the custom of sitting on the floor in front of those who were teaching God's Word. There were several speakers, and then my turn came. It was an honor to try to encourage leaders who daily faced the daunting task of proclaiming Jesus Christ in that mission field.

When my time of teaching ended, there was a fifteen-minute break, and we were all led to some long tables outside where we were offered bottles of water. As I sipped my water, one of my associates whispered that the man I had heard about was sitting at the far end of the table. I approached the man and slowly turned to face him so that I could greet him through my interpreter. It became evident that the story I had heard was true.

This brave young pastor had been preaching the gospel of Christ in a village somewhere in Bangladesh. God blessed his efforts, and a married Muslim woman accepted Jesus as Lord and Savior. Upon returning home to her nearby village, the woman informed her husband of her decision to be a Christian. Her husband exploded in anger. After threatening her, he secured a loaded pistol and went hunting for the pastor who had preached to his wife. The man found the pastor and, walking up to him as he was preaching, shot him multiple times in the face. Somehow this devoted pastor wasn't killed, but he was left severely wounded and needed urgent medical care.

When it was all over, and he had healed, this man of God, who was now facing me at the campground in Bangladesh, went right back to the village where he was shot, still proclaiming the love of God found in Jesus Christ. Talk about courage! As I looked at his scarred and disfigured face, it was hard to imagine such devotion to Jesus. Yet he was smiling and filled with the joy of the Lord.

Severe Testing

The apostle Paul also knew what it was to suffer for the name of Christ. As we learned earlier, he planted the church in Ephesus on one of his missionary journeys and lived there for three years. He served as a bondservant of Christ, with humility and tears. But there's more to the story: Paul did it all, he says, in the midst of "severe testing," stemming from the plots of his Jewish opponents. In other words, he carried out his ministry in the full knowledge that he was working amid enemies who were plotting to persecute and even kill him.

Now, I realize that all of us who serve the Lord have our battles, great and small. We all face occasional opposition. None of us wants to be disliked. Being attacked on social media is painful. But how many of us have had to face an environment where powerful people wanted to see us dead?

Paul, of course, had an example to follow for this very circumstance: Jesus faced the same situation. Even early in his ministry, he knew the Pharisees planned to kill him. When he healed the man with the shriveled hand—on the Sabbath, no less—Matthew tells us that "the Pharisees went out and plotted how they might kill Jesus. Aware of this, Jesus withdrew from that place" (Matt. 12:14–15). Note Matthew's statement that *Jesus was aware of the Pharisees' intentions.* He spent the rest of his life ministering in the full knowledge that his enemies hated him with a murderous rage. What kind of emotional strain did that make for the man who was perfectly God yet totally human?

A Treasure in Jars of Clay

Paul teaches us that, far from being extraordinary, the presence of obstacles and opposition is part and parcel of what it means to follow Jesus. And in those difficult situations, God is especially glorified through his faithful servants: "We have this treasure in jars of clay to show that this all-surpassing power is from God and not from us. We are *hard pressed* on every side, but not crushed; perplexed, but not *in despair*; persecuted, but not abandoned; *struck down*, but not destroyed. We always carry around in our body the death of Jesus, so that the life of Jesus may also be revealed in our body" (2 Cor. 4:7–10).

In other words, trouble and adversity are to be expected, and they make it plain to the world that any wisdom or strength we may demonstrate in our ministry comes from God, not from us.

Although most of us haven't had to go through what this pastor in Bangladesh had to endure, the truth is that there's suffering involved for all who serve the Lord. And leaders are Satan's special targets of attack. Carol and I have known our share. In the past I've written about our oldest girl, who walked away from God when she was about eighteen years old and had a baby out of wedlock. Often we didn't know where she was or what she was doing. I tried everything I could think of to remind her of how much we loved her, but my efforts only seemed to make matters worse. We went through a two-and-a-half-year nightmare. During this time, Carol had a serious medical crisis that affected her not only physically but mentally and emotionally as well, to the point that she spoke at times about not wanting to go on living.

Throughout all this, my nerves were shot. But I still had to get up in front of the congregation every week. And I knew they were going through their own problems. They didn't attend church on Sunday to hear about mine. Certainly there were people around us who loved and cared for us. But when people come to church, we can't focus on the hard season we're going through. They have their own trials and want to attend a service that lifts their spirits and brings them hope and encouragement.

We can't stand in front of people and say, "Good morning! It's great to see all of you. I'm glad you're here. But you know what? I've had a miserable week. Someone rear-ended my car, a pipe broke in the house, and the basement flooded. So I have nothing to say to you today. I had no time to study or pray. Have a great day. You're all dismissed." We can't do that. We're not allowed to mope because we've had a bad week. No matter what we face, we're called to walk through our difficulties with an attitude of "Look, I might be knocked down, but God has kept me from being knocked out."

What else do we learn from Paul's testimony? We learn that we can be perfectly in the center of God's will, anointed by the Holy Spirit, and still find ourselves surrounded by problems and confusion. In some American church circles, we are plagued by a false "dominion" or "victory" model of Christianity, which says that if you have faith and you're anointed, every door will fly open before you, obstacles will disappear, and your enemies will vanish. The implication is that if every door *isn't* flying open, if your obstacles *aren't* vanishing, then you must be doing something wrong. But that's not what God says. The examples of both Jesus and Paul make it clear that we can be in the center of God's will and still face severe trials. Paul told the Corinthians that he planned to stay in Ephesus for a time "because a great door for effective work has opened to me, and there are many who oppose me" (1 Cor. 16:9). Some translations say Paul planned to continue his work "*although* many oppose me" (NLT). Paul simply accepted opposition as part of his job.

And so must we. Carol and I have had many doors of opportunity open to us over the years, and guess what? With every door we've ever walked through, we've encountered adversaries, problems, financial shortages, letdowns—the list goes on and on. I don't doubt that you have your own list as well.

But let's look at Paul's list. Comparing himself with some self-styled "super-apostles" who were troubling the church in Corinth, Paul said,

> I have worked much harder, been in prison more frequently, been flogged more severely, and been exposed to death again and again. Five times I received from the Jews the forty lashes minus one. Three times I was beaten with rods, once I was pelted with stones, three times I was shipwrecked, I spent a night and a day in the open sea, I have been constantly on the move. I have been in danger from rivers, in danger from bandits, in danger from my fellow Jews, in danger from Gentiles; in danger in the city, in danger in the country, in danger at sea; and in danger from false believers. I have labored and toiled and have often gone without sleep; I have known hunger and thirst and have often gone without food; I have been cold and naked. Besides everything else, I face daily the pressure of my concern for all the churches. (2 Cor. 11:23–28)

What minister today would dare to admit such negative experiences? We've become mentally conditioned to see pain and trouble as signs of little faith or not being victorious. The point is not that we should compete for the longest list of trials and tribulations. Yet Paul boasted in the very circumstances we want to avoid at all costs: "If I must boast, I will boast of the things that show my weakness" (2 Cor. 11:30). Paul knew it was in his weakness that the strength of God was made perfect.

Recapturing Our Calling

One obstacle that every leader confronts is discouragement. I've often heard something like this: "Jim, can I tell you something?

I'm feeling defeated. I find myself in front of the church preaching, putting on a happy face, but inside I'm discouraged, worn down, wanting to walk away from it all. I don't know what to do. I'm at the end."

It happens to everyone. Sometimes Satan attacks and tries to take us out with a single blow. But most of the time, his strategy is simply to keep us under the pressure of financial, pastoral, and family concerns—hour after hour, day after day, week after week, month after month. His strategy is to weaken us and tire us out until eventually we crumble. I call it the run-around, run-down, run-away syndrome. We *run around* preaching, teaching, and helping people until we are spiritually *run down* and soon want to *run away* from it all.

We're in good company. Remember the story of Elijah? After a long series of spiritual battles, he received word from Jezebel that she intended to kill him. Here's what happened next:

> Elijah was afraid and ran for his life. When he came to Beersheba in Judah, he left his servant there, while he himself went a day's journey into the wilderness. He came to a broom bush, sat down under it and prayed that he might die. "I have had enough, Lord," he said. "Take my life; I am no better than my ancestors." Then he lay down under the bush and fell asleep.
>
> All at once an angel touched him and said, "Get up and eat." He looked around, and there by his head was some bread baked over hot coals, and a jar of water. He ate and drank and then lay down again.
>
> The angel of the Lord came back a second time and touched him and said, "Get up and eat, for the journey is too much for you." So he got up and ate and drank. Strengthened by that food, he traveled forty days and forty nights until he reached Horeb, the mountain of God. (1 Kings 19:3–8)

How could Elijah be God's mighty prophet and yet run for his life when Jezebel threatened him? He was human.

But notice what happened.

First, God sent an angel to minister to Elijah. The lesson is that even when we are at our lowest, God is mindful of our situation and will come to our aid.

Second, the angel brought Elijah bread and water. Elijah ate and drank and then lay down. This provides good advice on how to take care of our bodies. Nourishment and rest strengthen us. An older minister once told me, "Jim, remember this: sometimes God's perfect will for us is to take a nap." Biblical commentators also believe the nourishment that the angel provided for Elijah was likely a symbol of the spiritual food we need—shutting ourselves away, immersing ourselves in the Word, drinking deeply from the Spirit of God.

Third, Elijah was restored to the point that he was able to travel forty days and forty nights to Mount Horeb, where God spoke to him in a "gentle whisper" (1 Kings 19:12) and then gave Elijah a personal word of instruction as to what to do next.

God did something similar when Paul was planting a church in Corinth. Amid the opposition that always seemed to plague the apostle, the Lord spoke to him in a vision at night: "Do not be afraid; keep on speaking, do not be silent. For I am with you, and no one is going to attack and harm you, because I have many people in this city" (Acts 18:9–10).

As a result, Paul stayed in Corinth for another year and a half, building up and strengthening the church there. A personal word from the Lord helped Paul overcome fear and spiritual fatigue. This wasn't a new doctrine or another truth to be added to Scripture. It was a specific word from the Lord for his faithful servant only while he was in Corinth. Elsewhere Paul was attacked regularly and suffered harm.

In a similar vein, Timothy received personal words from God about his gifting and calling, which Paul reminded him about in later years: "Timothy, my son, I am giving you this command in keeping with the prophecies once made about you, so that by recalling them you may fight the battle well" (1 Tim. 1:18) and "Do not neglect your gift, which was given you through prophecy when the body of elders laid their hands on you" (1 Tim. 4:14).

Remembering the call and gifting that God placed on our lives at the beginning of our ministries often provides powerful inspiration so we can "fight the battle well" (1 Tim. 1:18). Has God ever impressed your heart with a similar personal word? Was there ever a moment in seminary or Bible school or in your devotions when you felt that God gave you a prophetic intimation of what he wanted to do through you? Sometimes we miss out on our calling not because God has changed his mind but because we get so tired, perplexed, and discouraged that we lose sight of it. But let's remember our calling right now and ask God to restore it in our hearts. We can recapture our calling and pray with David, "Remember your word to your servant, for you have given me hope" (Ps. 119:49).

Renewed Day by Day

What's the secret? How did Paul find strength and perseverance through all his adversity, and what can we learn from what he went through? Let's look at his own words: "Therefore we do not lose heart. Though outwardly we are wasting away, yet *inwardly* we are being renewed *day by day*. For our light and momentary troubles are achieving for us an eternal glory that far outweighs them all. So we fix our eyes not on what is seen, but on what is unseen, since what is seen is temporary, but what is unseen is eternal" (2 Cor. 4:16–18).

Paul's secret was that he was renewed spiritually "day by day." Not week by week or month by month. *Day by day.*

Over the years, the Lord has made this passage a real help to me. Following Jesus is always a day-by-day proposition. Remember the manna in the desert? The Israelites were in dire straits. They didn't have enough to eat, and they grumbled against Moses and Aaron. The Lord said to Moses, "I will rain down bread from heaven for you. The people are to go out each day and gather enough for that day" (Ex. 16:4).

The day-by-day nature of God's provision was important. *Each day* the people were to gather enough manna for *that day.* Moses told them that except for taking two days' worth of manna on the sixth day so that they could rest on the Sabbath, no one was to keep any of the manna until morning (Ex. 16:19). When some of the people ignored this directive and kept a portion of one day's manna overnight, they found in the morning that it was "full of maggots and began to smell" (Ex. 16:20).

This principle carries over into the New Testament. Jesus himself, when he taught the disciples how to pray, said, "Give us today our *daily* bread" (Matt. 6:11).

Today Is Everything

God's grace works the same way. Each day, God gives us what we need for that day. Yesterday's manna won't get us through today. Today's manna won't get us through tomorrow. It's not like a car, where we can fill the tank one day and drive all week. Following Jesus is about today. It's about right now. Yesterday is gone. We can't change it. And we may never see tomorrow. Many of us go through life embittered by what has happened in the past or fearful of what might happen in the future. But when we're focused on yesterday or worried about tomorrow, our *today* quickly goes by, and we miss its opportunities and God's promised provision. Today is the only day we have. It's the only day in which we can fulfill God's will and bring him glory.

Again, when can we hear God and follow his voice? Yesterday? Too late. Tomorrow? Not yet. Today is everything. When the Israelites followed the tabernacle through the desert, their only itinerary was to follow the cloud day by day. When the cloud moved, they moved; when it stopped, so did they. "As long as the cloud stayed over the tabernacle, they remained in camp. . . . Sometimes the cloud stayed only from evening till morning, and when it lifted in the morning, they set out. Whether by day or by night, whenever the cloud lifted, they set out" (Num. 9:18, 21). When can we repent and seek forgiveness? When can we dig deeper into the Word? When can we exchange our weakness for God's strength? Today is the only day available to us. That's why Paul said we need to be inwardly renewed day by day. Furthermore, today is the only day we have to spread the gospel. "I tell you, now is the time of God's favor, now is the day of salvation" (2 Cor. 6:2).

What does it mean, as a practical matter, to be renewed every day? How we define it, and how we go about it, is deeply personal and will likely be different for each of us. I like to think of George Müller, the famous man of faith and director of Ashley Down orphanage in Bristol, England. God directed him to never ask for money. So for decades he fed and clothed hundreds, sometimes thousands, of children, not knowing how the bills would be paid. Imagine waking up in the morning knowing you have several hundred hungry children to feed, and you have only enough food for breakfast. Nothing for lunch or dinner. Müller said, "I saw more clearly than ever, that the first great and primary business to which I ought to attend every day was, to have my soul happy in the Lord."[1] And he achieved this by starting every day alone with the Lord, asking him to speak to him through his Word and in prayer. Like Müller, we must find our own way to be inwardly renewed each new day. We must receive fresh strength by being alone with Jesus, unrushed and with a listening heart.

Daily Refill

Another problem common to the ministry is that of exhaustion—physical, mental, or spiritual. Many of us feel like we're running on empty most of the time. I remember when we realized it was time for our church to move out of the remodeled theater building we'd been meeting in for years. It was bursting at the seams, and sometimes people had to be turned away. This dismayed me and caused me to consult our pastoral staff about seeking a bigger space as soon as possible. I naively thought it would take only about eighteen months to find a new building and move in. Wrong. We ended up having to add a fourth service on Sundays to accommodate more people. Now it was nine o'clock, noon, three o'clock, and six o'clock. Each service was about two hours long. We did that for *six years.* Carol and I were so tired by the end of those days that when we turned off the car in front of our home, we wondered whether we had the strength to make it upstairs. I would wake up exhausted every Monday morning.

The question we all have to answer is, Where do *we* go to get spiritually renewed? We pour ourselves out for others. Who's pouring into *us*? We call people to church on Sunday so we can feed them the Word of God. But who's feeding *us*?

For me to be renewed every day, I have to receive something fresh from the Lord. I start with the Bible because that's paramount, but it has to be made alive by the Holy Spirit and personalized in my heart. Remember, the Pharisees knew more Old Testament doctrine and verses than anyone, and yet they were the ones who plotted Jesus's death. The Word has to become food for my soul, and I have to meet God in prayer.

I ask the Lord to minister to my heart through his Holy Spirit. Where is Jesus right now? Seated at the right hand of the Father. He's coming back, but before he left, he promised to send us the Holy Spirit. And the Spirit himself has come to renew our hearts through the Word every single day. Notice that renewal is an inward experience. The condition of our innermost spirit is everything. We can exercise regularly and eat healthy foods; and although these are good habits, they are of no help to the inner being that determines our spiritual strength and vitality.

My own practice is to have something of a church service just for myself. I go somewhere I can be alone. I listen to Christian music. I even sing along. I read and meditate on Scripture. (I do everything but take an offering.) I often read one or two sermons that I gather from my library—I need the Word ministered to me just as the congregation does on Sundays. And I spend time in prayer. When I'm done, I find I am spiritually renewed.

Living in the Future, Living in the Invisible

Here on planet earth, we live in the natural, physical realm—the realm of what our five senses can perceive. And it can often overwhelm us. Before we've even finished breakfast, we have possibly been inundated with bad news, gossip, anxiety—problems of all kinds. The obstacles and opposition we face in our ministries only compound the problem. How do we overcome all that?

Daily spiritual renewal has everything to do with our faith being reinvigorated. The author of the letter to the Hebrews wrote, "Faith is confidence in what we *hope* for and assurance about what we *do not see*" (Heb. 11:1). Faith is the ability of the soul to perceive things not revealed to the senses. When our hearts and minds are renewed, when our faith is quickened, God lifts us out of the merely physical world and into the spiritual realm, where he wants us to live.

We learn from this verse that faith allows us to step beyond the physical realm in two ways. First, faith lifts us into the realm of the future: *"confidence in what we hope for."* Hope always speaks about the future. For example, the confidence we have as Christians that Jesus will return one day is called the blessed *hope* of the church. When we're filled with faith, we're strongly influenced by and confident about *everything* God says about the future—the end of the world, our soul's destiny, heaven, and the rewards that await the believer. And that confidence then affects how we live in the here and now.

By faith Abraham left his home and the only culture he knew and traveled at God's command, even though "he did not know where he was going" (Heb. 11:8). How can one leave everything behind with no solid plans, no GPS for guidance, and no guarantees except God's call? Upon reaching the promised land, "he lived in tents" (Heb. 11:9), indicating that Abraham would always be a stranger in any earthly country. Why? Because his faith caused him to look into the future with the solid hope that there was a city waiting for him, one "with foundations, whose architect and builder is God" (Heb. 11:10). That kind of faith in God, which risks everything, has been the inspiration behind the amazing exploits and sacrifices made by servants of God throughout church history. Oh, God, increase our faith!

Second, faith carries us into the realm of the invisible: *"assurance about what we do not see."* The physical senses can't perceive the existence of the soul, the person of the Holy Spirit, or the call of God on our lives. But faith can make those things more real to us than the chair we're sitting on. That's what living by faith is all about—the soul perceiving the future and the invisible as more real than the physical world around it. This kind of real faith brings joy to God's heart. "Without faith it is impossible to please God, because anyone who comes to him must believe that he exists and that he rewards those who earnestly seek him" (Heb. 11:6).

When Jesus was on earth, he lived in the reality of future things and the realm of what he could not see. That's how he was able to transcend the trials and tribulations of his earthly life. That's also how Paul overcame the fierce opposition he faced. Remember how he emphasized that he lived "by faith, not by sight" (2 Cor. 5:7)? Living daily under the influence of God's promises for the future and the Lord's invisible presence around him is what brought Paul through. If God was able to do that for Paul, don't you think he's able to help us overcome the "light and momentary troubles" (2 Cor. 4:17) we face as leaders?

We need to face our situations honestly, with the help of God. "Burnout" has become the complaint of so many church leaders that we've accepted it without digging a little deeper. Paul the Apostle worked harder than any of us and often faced death. He was beaten half to death, shipwrecked, and constantly on the move. He was no stranger to nakedness, hunger, and thirst as he labored over decades for his Master. And yet he had not one word of complaint or a hint of burnout!

I don't want to diminish the challenges and hardships you face right now as you fulfill your calling. But can we humbly consider the possibility that Paul lived off spiritual resources found in Christ that we have yet to discover? Isn't there strength from God's Word and power from the Holy Spirit yet untapped by most of us? God's will is not for us to burn out but to burn *on* for his glory. "He who began a good work in you will carry it on to completion until the day of Christ Jesus" (Phil. 1:6).

CHAPTER 4

NOT ASHAMED OF
THE GOSPEL

I have declared to both Jews and Greeks that
they must turn to God in repentance and have
faith in our Lord Jesus.

—ACTS 20:21

Louisiana State Penitentiary—known as "Angola"—is the largest maximum-security prison in the United States. It is named after the former slave plantation that once occupied the site, which in turn drew its name from the African nation of Angola, the origin of many slaves brought to Louisiana in the nineteenth century. The prison occupies about 18,000 acres—larger than the size of Manhattan—and houses some 6,300 inmates. Up to 97 percent of the inmates are serving life sentences.[1] Angola has long been notorious for brutality, riots, escapes, and murder. For many years it was known as "America's bloodiest prison."

Angola may seem an unlikely place for the gospel to take hold. But it has.

In 1995 a man named Burl Cain became the warden at

Angola. Three months after he arrived, he presided over his first execution. Before the execution, Burl spoke with the condemned man. The man cursed Angola, cursed Louisiana, cursed his mother, cursed his father, cursed God, cursed the day he was born—he basically went into eternity cursing. Burl's mother, who had raised him as a Christian, said to him, "Son, God put you there for a reason. You'd better do something." And he did. He supervised the building of small chapels among the various yards and camps that make up the complex. The well-known book *Experiencing God* by Henry Blackaby and my own (considerably less well-known) book *Fresh Wind, Fresh Fire* were circulated among the inmates. Slowly, inmates received Christ and the chapel attendance grew. Larger churches were built, representing various Christian traditions. In the 1990s Angola partnered with the New Orleans Baptist Theological Seminary to give prisoners the opportunity to earn degrees in ministry.

In 2008 Carol and I were invited to visit Angola. We were asked to bring the Brooklyn Tabernacle Singers to give a concert in the ten-thousand-seat stadium where the Angola Prison Rodeo is held every year. Carol had long had it in her heart to involve the Singers in prison ministry, and we readily accepted the invitation. On an oppressively hot Saturday in August, several thousand inmates, each of whom had to ask for and receive special clearance to attend, took their places in the stadium. The Singers gave a concert, and I shared the gospel. It was a special day of ministry. The best part was meeting a number of inmates who had become Christians during their time in Angola. Their stories were amazing.

One of the inmates was a man named Greg, who in former times had worshiped Satan in the cellblock where he was housed. The hopelessness of his situation became so overwhelming that he decided to make a rope and hang himself. But then a darker idea occurred to him. He would get some leftover iron plate from the metal-working shop and make an axe from it. His plan, he said, was to walk from one part of the prison to another and "make a mess" out of everyone he encountered "until they put a bullet in my head." Before he could carry out his horrific plan, Greg providentially received a pass to visit one of the chapels on the Angola grounds. It just so happened that one of the chaplains was there at the time. As Greg tells the story, "Twenty minutes later I was lying facedown on the floor, and I gave my life to the Lord. A week later I was baptized, and I've never looked back." He still has the number 666 tattooed on his chest. He wears it, he says, "as a testimony to who I'm not anymore."[2]

Everyone has heard of a "jailhouse conversion," where an inmate who isn't sincere begins "talking the talk" in hopes of persuading the parole board to give him an early release. The conversions I've seen in Angola aren't like that. Very few prisoners are ever released from Angola. The average sentence is over ninety years.[3] They have no reason to think that "getting religion" will magically change their circumstances. I led one man to Christ who had been kept in the same cell twenty-three hours a day for more than twenty-five years. He has since been released into the general population, but more importantly, he is a new creation through Jesus Christ.

Visiting a place like Angola highlights basic spiritual realities with such stark clarity: life, death, heaven, hell, Satan, Jesus, sin, repentance, salvation. There are few subtleties. It's a matter of receiving Christ as Savior or spending eternity without him. The difference is one thing and one thing only: accepting the gospel of Jesus Christ.

As we continue with Paul's words to the Ephesian church leaders, we find him reminding them of these basic spiritual realities: "I have declared to both Jews and Greeks that they must turn to God in repentance and have faith in our Lord Jesus" (Acts 20:21). Note the word *must*. For Paul there was no question, no doubt, no alternative.

It is also noteworthy that Paul told "both Jews and Greeks"—that is, *everyone*, regardless of race, ethnicity, or social status—that they had to turn to God. So the message of freedom in Christ is not just for some inmate who has no hope of ever walking free again. Some people may look as if they're free, but they're in a prison of their own making. The stark alternatives of freedom versus prison so evident in Angola are no different for the people we meet every day. Except, in most cases, they're blinded by the idols of pleasure-seeking and materialism. We must be faithful to Christ and present the gospel so everyone can know the freedom Jesus gives.

One Soul at a Time

It's a depressing sign of the state of the church today that we need to be reminded of these simple realities. Everyone we encounter has an eternal destiny. And the gospel of Christ is the only way to salvation. But are Christian leaders and churches clear on these facts? What is one to think when the Barna Group reports that more than half (51 percent) of churchgoers have never heard of the Great Commission to "go into all the world and preach the gospel to all creation" (Mark 16:15)? Only 17 percent of church-goers are familiar with that passage, and another 25 percent say they have heard of it but don't know what it means.[4]

We often wring our hands about modern culture, secular humanism, and who is in the White House. It's as if the Christian church were helpless. But in this mindset we are sadly misguided. The early church faced a culture that was as anti-God as anything we face today, and yet the number of believers multiplied. How? By believers simply sharing the gospel of Jesus Christ.

In Acts 6 and 7 we read the account of Stephen, the first martyr of the church. "A man full of God's grace and power" (Acts 6:8), he was falsely accused of blasphemy. After a sham trial during which Stephen provided as his defense a historical overview of Israel through to "the coming of [Jesus] the Righteous One" (Acts 7:52), he was stoned and killed. "On that day a great persecution broke out against the church in Jerusalem, and all except the apostles were scattered throughout Judea and Samaria. . . . Those who had been scattered preached the word wherever they went" (Acts 8:1, 4).

Notice that everyone was scattered *except* the apostles. But everywhere the believers went, they shared the gospel. And that's how the church multiplied. It wasn't the ministry of the apostles alone that caused the growth. Everyone who was scattered effectively became an evangelist.

Think what it would mean for our churches today if every member consistently proclaimed the good news of Jesus. If a third of the people brought just one soul to church in five months, and another third brought a soul in the next five months, and so on, every church would soon need a new building!

Look at the Fields

When Jesus first called his disciples, he said to them, "Come, follow me . . . and I will send you out to fish for people" (Matt. 4:19). That was the disciples' primary mission: to save souls.

It's our primary mission as well.

Have you ever asked yourself, "Why are we still here?" The Lord has saved us. We're going to heaven one day. So why aren't we in heaven already? If Jesus wants to take us home, why doesn't he do it now? Why leave us here, struggling with sin and temptation and hardship?

The main reason we're still here is to "fish" for men and women. That's God's purpose for Christians here on earth. In heaven, we will still worship (although seeing the Lord face-to-face will far exceed what we experience here). But there will be no soul-winning to do, for every soul in heaven is there because of faith in Christ. "Fishing for souls" is the one thing we need to do *now*. But how much time, effort, and prayer do our churches devote to it? How often do we preach the good news? How effectively do we train our people to share it?

It's critically important that we come to see the world the way the Lord sees it. Three repeated yet slightly different passages in the gospel narratives provide some insight. The repetition of this teaching is meant to highlight its vital importance. Let's look at each of the three passages.

Matthew describes Jesus going through all the towns and villages, teaching and preaching, healing people, casting out demons, raising a young girl from the dead, and giving sight to a blind man. He was surrounded by people pressing him on all sides, trying to get his attention. "When he saw the crowds, he had compassion on them, because they were harassed and helpless, like sheep without a shepherd. Then he said to his disciples, 'The harvest is plentiful but the workers are few. Ask the Lord of the harvest, therefore, to send out workers into his harvest field'" (Matt. 9:36–38).

Jesus saw the people as "harassed and helpless." Another translation says he saw them as "torn" (Rotherham); yet another as "mangled" (Berkeley). They had been beaten down by life and their own sins. They knew of no one to turn to for help and deliverance. But Jesus had compassion on them. The harvest was plentiful. But, he said, "the workers are few." Notice what he didn't say. He didn't say, "The worshipers are few." He didn't say, "The churchgoers are few." He said, "The *workers* are few." That was the critical shortage. There weren't enough workers to accomplish this great task that weighed on Jesus's heart. Oddly, even though almighty, the Lord declares his need for workers to reap the harvest. If that weren't true, why point out the lack of them?

The gospel of Luke presents the same message from a different perspective.

"The Lord appointed seventy-two others and sent them two by two ahead of him to every town and place where he was about to go. He told them, 'The harvest is plentiful, but the workers are few. Ask the Lord of the harvest, therefore, to send out workers into his harvest field'" (Luke 10:1–2). Jesus spoke these words to a group of his followers who were going "ahead of him" to prepare the way for his visit. When we see someone come to Christ—a life transformed by grace—we know that some "worker" somewhere, somehow, shared the gospel, along with loving and praying in such a way that the person put their trust in Jesus. According to Christ himself, those workers are necessary for his kingdom to be extended.

Both Matthew's and Luke's accounts tell us that Jesus told his followers to *ask* the Lord to send out workers. One might wonder why it needs to work that way. Couldn't God raise up the workers and send them out himself? Why does he need us to ask him to do it? Part of the reason is that the Lord has chosen to partner with us in building his church. In Christ alone are forgiveness of sin and salvation, yet God commissions simple believers to declare the message—not angels or a voice from heaven. Notice that Jesus didn't say to train workers first; instead, he asked them to pray that the Lord would raise them up and send them out. Ultimately only God can equip and empower the workers needed to build the kingdom. Formal Bible training can be useful, yet his first disciples never attended seminary. But the Holy Spirit still used them mightily in the fields ripe for harvest. Church history has shown us that it's not learned theologians but rather simple believers who do most of the harvesting for Jesus.

John's rendition of the passage brings out yet another aspect of harvesting: "Don't you have a saying, 'It's still four months until harvest'? I tell you, open your eyes and look at the fields! They are ripe for harvest" (John 4:35). Farming has different times and seasons for different tasks: plant in the spring, nurture through the summer, harvest in the fall. But here, Jesus is saying, "Look! The harvest is ready *now*. Do the work today. Tomorrow will be too late for many of the 'harassed and helpless' multitudes." His question to his disciples then, and to us today, is this: Why do you wait?

Preaching for Conversions

Have you noticed that Paul always preached for conversions? He wasn't an example of "pastor as life coach." He didn't look to help people spruce up their résumés so that they could get better jobs or give pep talks to improve their self-image. Of course, it's good to help people better their life circumstances. But that's not what Paul was primarily about. Paul lived to make converts. Everything else was secondary. Remember: when he first came to Ephesus, no one there knew who he was. They didn't know who Jesus was. There was no advance team. The Ephesians didn't have Christian parents or grandparents whose legacy he could remind them of. Paul was on his own, preaching a message people had never heard before about a Savior they had never heard of and a salvation they could never have imagined.

Paul was "driven" to make converts. But it was the heart of Christ that drove him. I've studied church history enough to know that all the great soul-winners were the same way. My late friend Dave Wilkerson, who founded Teen Challenge, once observed that God never seemed to work through a man or woman until they got "a little bit crazy"—in other words, radical—about leading others to Jesus. No one can inject that kind of passion into us. Only God can. Something divine needs to happen inside us, making us discontent unless we see people coming to Christ. Otherwise we can grow complacent and accept "what is," rather than seeing "what could be" through God. The ministry isn't just a job. It's a sacred calling. We don't just preach sermons and lead services and then collect a paycheck. We deal with eternal life and eternal judgment. Paul preached for converts. So must we.

Learning from the Sermons in Acts

Let me recommend an exercise for you—one I've done many times and have found to be extremely helpful. Go through the book of Acts and read every sermon recorded there. And don't just read the sermons—analyze them. Carefully observe the sentence structures. What's the subject? What's the verb? What's the object? Peter preached a sermon on the day of Pentecost that resulted in three thousand people getting saved (Acts 2:14–41). Could we possibly learn something from that sermon? For example, at the end of the sermon, he says, "Repent and be baptized . . . in the name of Jesus Christ for the forgiveness of your sins. And you will receive the gift of the Holy Spirit" (Acts 2:38). You can't reduce the good news down to anything better than that. A short time later Peter preached again after healing a lame man: "You killed the author of life, but God raised him from the dead. . . . Repent, then, and turn to God" (Acts 3:15, 19). Notice the bold, confrontational nature of his appeal as he shares the message of the cross. Does that describe our messages and ministries?

The book of Acts records these gospel messages that God wanted us to study and learn from. What did they say that we're not saying today? What did they *not* say that we tend to focus on? Paul wrote about many important spiritual subjects in his letters to Christian churches, but they were not part of his message to unbelievers. Are we emphasizing secondary doctrinal issues that were not part of Paul's message of salvation? Worse, are we adding completely extraneous matters that distract from the gospel message that he preached? Notice, for example, that Paul never included a "join our church" element. Nor did he promote a particular denomination. We must always keep in mind the awesome warning that Paul gave about preaching "another gospel": "Even if we or an angel from heaven should preach a gospel other than the one we preached to you, let them be under God's curse! As we have already said, so now I say again: If anybody is preaching to you a gospel other than what you accepted, let them be under God's curse!" (Gal. 1:8–9).

Christ commissioned all of us to proclaim the gospel. It's not an option; it's a command. But we must be sure it's the gospel found in Scripture and not one we've added to or subtracted from.

Notice please that Paul preached the same gospel to everyone—Jews or gentiles, it didn't matter. They all heard the same good news about salvation through Jesus Christ. Every Jew and every gentile could receive salvation only through faith in Christ. There is still only that one gospel. There is not a Black gospel or a White gospel. There's not one gospel for millennials and another for senior citizens. There is only the gospel of Jesus Christ. Times change and cultures might differ, but the message remains the same.

In every sermon we preach, in every teaching we give, we ultimately need to get to Jesus because he alone is the Savior of the world and the image of the invisible God. Only in Christ do we find life and salvation. Of course, we also preach from the Old Testament. We can preach about Moses or Elijah, from the

Psalms or the historical books. There are good lessons there. But we have to somehow make our way back to Jesus and the cross, or the sermon will be powerless. Remember, God has made a *new* covenant, immeasurably better than the *old* one:

> If there had been nothing wrong with that first covenant, no place would have been sought for another. But God found fault with the people and said:
>
> > The days are coming, declares the Lord,
> >   when I will make a new covenant
> > with the people of Israel
> >   and with the people of Judah.
> > It will not be like the covenant
> >   I made with their ancestors
> > when I took them by the hand
> >   to lead them out of Egypt,
> > because they did not remain faithful to my
> >   covenant,
> >   and I turned away from them,
> >   declares the Lord. (Heb. 8:7–9)

Notice that the new covenant centered on Jesus Christ would "not be like the covenant" made through Moses. We must always keep that in mind and use the old covenant only as a figure and precursor of the new where it applies. Paul confirms this as he summarizes his message: "*He* is the one we proclaim, admonishing and teaching everyone with all wisdom, so that we may present everyone fully mature *in Christ*" (Col. 1:28). The life of Joshua can't save anyone. The demons don't flee when we cry, "Elijah!" or even when we say "God" or "Creator" or "the Holy One." But they certainly do tremble when we invoke the name of

Jesus! I can't imagine that Peter or Paul ever preached a sermon that wasn't ultimately—if not entirely—about Jesus and God's new covenant.

Add Nothing, Subtract Nothing

Our lack of gospel preaching has done great harm. We have to preach the gospel, the whole gospel, and nothing but the gospel. We can't add anything, and we can't subtract anything. If we do, it's no longer the gospel.

Let's use an analogy from everyday life. My wife, Carol, makes an amazing spaghetti sauce. She's followed the same recipe for years. If she left out the garlic, the sauce wouldn't taste the same. Same goes for the fresh basil. And if someone sneaked into the kitchen and added some cinnamon, it wouldn't taste the same either. It might be sweeter, but no longer "her" sauce. It's the same with the gospel. God has given it to us in its complete and perfect form. He doesn't need creative input from me or you.

When it comes to the gospel, a friend once told me, "If it's true, it's not new. If it's new, it's not true." If we add something or subtract something, it's not the same gospel. If we tweak it to make it more palatable to the secular culture, it's not the same gospel. You might say, "But everyone's doing it!" What does it matter? Do we want to follow passing fads, or do we want to be faithful to Christ? Some say, "But it's a new day!" *Every* day is a new day. But every day is *still* "the day of salvation" (2 Cor. 6:2), and salvation comes only through the one gospel of Christ. Are so-called experts saying God can't do today what he did before? This is the cancer eating away at the vitals of Christian churches: unbelief in the power of Christ for today.

It goes without saying that we dare not preach any false gospel. But the tragic reality is that many leaders today give messages which, while not directly denying the gospel, nevertheless make additions or subtractions or modifications that weaken or even distort it. If we don't preach the full, unadulterated gospel, we won't see converts. The gospel alone, without any added help from us, "is the power of God that brings salvation to everyone who believes" (Rom. 1:16).

Many sneer at the gospel's crude simplicity or its confrontational nature. Others mock it as shallow emotionalism. But look around at the state of the world and the condition of the church and explain to me the improvements we've made by departing from the gospel. The truth is, we're not seeing enough transformed lives. Will fads get people to come to our churches? Quite possibly. We could fill a building. The sad fact is that many of us have filled our buildings with people who aren't Christians in the New Testament sense. We're seeing the results of our drift from the gospel not only in a more pagan culture but also in the sad spiritual state of the contemporary church.

The Sunday Morning Mission Field

I once spoke to a group about God's desire for us to win souls. A man in the front row blurted out, "Yeah, but what if half your congregation isn't saved?" It's a question we might prefer not to ask ourselves, but we need to face facts. If people in our churches attend only once or twice monthly, want the shortest meetings possible, have no appetite for prayer, and aren't interested in spiritual things, something is wrong. If they know more about how to use their phones than their New Testament but then say they want to go to heaven for eternity, we have to stop and ask ourselves, "What has my preaching and ministry produced? Are these folks genuinely Christian?" They never will be unless we present to them the message of Jesus, who said, "You must be born again"

(John 3:7). Expecting spiritual growth from people who have not experienced the new birth is a waste of time. Preaching to them about principles and morality found in the Bible only makes them hard-hearted and even more self-righteous.

The purpose of the gospel is to convert people to Christ, not to get them to say, "I'm going to try to live a better life," or to get them to come back the following Sunday. And certainly the goal should not be to have them merely recite some words. I once visited a church where the pastor preached an insipid sermon without much Jesus in it and, at the end of the service, said, "Before we dismiss, let's everybody pray this prayer together: 'Dear God, thank you for loving me. I receive Jesus as my Savior. Amen.'" And then he exclaimed, "You are now all Christians." No mention of the sin that nailed Jesus to the cross, no mention of what repentance means. Shallow ministry won't make saints out of sinners.

If our people haven't been born again, we have to preach to them, pray for them, agonize over them. We must love them and some way, somehow bring them to Christ. Sometimes an overlooked mission field is sitting right in front of us on Sunday morning.

But how can we pastors complain about our congregations' spiritual condition if we're their spiritual leaders? If the Brooklyn Tabernacle were filled with people who came to church every week but weren't believers in Jesus, that would be my responsibility, in some sense. I'm the shepherd. What kind of messages am I preaching? What kind of spiritual food am I providing? Is the Holy Spirit helping me? My wife and I made a vow to each other a long time ago. Thousands of people come to the Brooklyn Tabernacle every Sunday, and we're grateful for that. But we'll go back to our first building with one hundred people in the pews if we have to, as long as they're true believers. What value is there in having a building filled with people singing and swaying to the music, while knowing they don't really know Christ as Savior? I wouldn't be able to sleep at night. Paul could sleep at night. Why? Because he gave the full, unadulterated gospel to everyone and saw them become new creations through the grace of God in Jesus Christ.

A major question facing Christian leaders today is, Who is sitting in front of me week after week? We must be aware that even those who often attend the services might not know Christ. Imagine all the people who may have been going to the temple in Jesus's day with no idea about who God really was. That would include religious leaders who preached about the Messiah yet had the Messiah five feet away and didn't recognize him. There could likewise be churchgoers today who call themselves Christians but don't know the Lord.

I'm reminded of the parable of the lost coin: "Suppose a woman has ten silver coins and loses one. Doesn't she light a lamp, sweep the house and search carefully until she finds it? And when she finds it, she calls her friends and neighbors together and says, 'Rejoice with me; I have found my lost coin'" (Luke 15:8–9).

Notice that the woman's coin was lost *in* the house. This is a reminder that we must keep watch over our flocks and not take for granted that they are all Christians.

In the end, we have a choice. We can either lead people to Christ and see them grow spiritually or we can dilute the message so that people are comfortable living in their sin. When we come before the Lord to give an account of our ministries, we do not want to hear Jesus say, "I gave my life so that sins could be forgiven. And you didn't share the meaning of my cross and resurrection? How could your only goal be to get them back the next Sunday!"

Preaching to the Saved?

This concern raises another important question. What does our preaching mean for the members of the church—hopefully the majority—who *are* saved? How do we preach a message that will feed the believers but still reach the unbelievers? If we go all one way, or all the other, we risk leaving someone out. We always need to be mindful of the people attending who still need to meet Jesus. We must give the gospel to the guy in the balcony who's strung out on cocaine. Or the woman bound by oxycodone. Or the businessman who tries to live a moral life but doesn't know the Savior. They all need to hear the good news of salvation through Jesus.

But where does that leave the rest of the congregation? They already know the gospel message. They already *are* saved. They need to learn more about love. They need to know the possibilities of faith. They need instruction about the person and work of the Holy Spirit. They need to know about the second coming of the Lord and other blessings of the new covenant. But the unbelievers in the audience will not fully appreciate any of that. "The person without the Spirit does not accept the things that come from the Spirit of God but considers them foolishness, and cannot understand them because they are discerned only through the Spirit" (1 Cor. 2:14). So how do we preach in a way that meets everyone's needs? It's not easy, but the Spirit will help us. Let me share something I've learned.

Let's say I'm preaching from 1 Corinthians 13 about the supremacy of agape love. I try to establish that it's more important than faith, understanding spiritual mysteries, even doctrinal knowledge. But I know the characteristics of love that follow in the text are too numerous for the heart and mind to take in at once.

Many of our sermons have too many outline points. When

we present our people with loads of points and information, we risk having none of what we say truly pierce the heart. When a preacher says, "Point nine . . . ," it probably won't be very effective. It might be doctrinally sound and true, but who can appreciate and digest so much food at one sitting? As Samuel Chadwick said, "The further you get from simplicity, the further you get from God."[5]

Warren Wiersbe once suggested that when we prepare a sermon, the truth we want to communicate should be narrowed down to a sentence or two. That way we can leave people with the main thought of the message. Also, before we go off on a tangent regarding some obscure topic, we need to ask ourselves, "Does anyone really care?" A preacher might have a fascination with the origin of the Philistines or where Cain got his wife. But I think we can agree that those have little connection with our audience, who daily face spiritual battles and problems of all kinds.

In addition to keeping our message simple, every sermon should also include a call to action. In other words, what response does this truth from God call for? Repent and receive Christ? Believe God for more grace in your life? Be encouraged? Come to the throne of grace in prayer? Give thanks in everything? Sometimes the preacher eloquently provides a lot of information and walks off to applause. But if we don't call people to act on God's truth right then and there, they will likely forget the sermon before they get home.

Because of the need for clarity, when I'm preaching, say from 1 Corinthians 13, I focus on something simple. I might focus on "love is patient, love is kind." Being patient and kind to those around us is often a challenge, but that's the very testing ground of God's love in us through the Holy Spirit. I try to point out that agape love is the only measuring stick as to our spiritual maturity, and not verses memorized or theological propositions understood. D. L. Moody once said somewhere that the hardest thing for God to do is make someone kind. Once I've explained the passage, the hardest part is still ahead. How do I make a personal application of these truths to the people in front of me in a tender but challenging way? "You know, folks, it's not how we act in church only. Can our family member say we exhibit God's kindness at home every day? Do the people who work with us see God's patience in our lives?"

We need wisdom from the Holy Spirit to apply the sermon because that's where the rubber meets the road. Conviction, repentance, and prayer for mercy are liberating for those of us in the light of God's truth. But how about the unbelievers who are listening to all this? We must never forget them, and one of the challenges in preaching is to take the application for believers and turn that into an illustration of the love of God in the gospel of Jesus Christ.

Here's how I once ended a message on patience and kindness:

> Well, I've been talking about love, patience, and kindness in the Christian life, but I want to finish by telling you about someone who is ultimate love. God so loved this world that he sent his Son Jesus Christ to die for your sins and mine, even before we were born. That is the ultimate expression of patience and kindness. That's how much God loves you. Even if you don't want him, he wants *you*. Even if you don't believe in him, he loves you. He brought you here today. He wants to show his love to you. He has a gift for you, the gift of eternal life. Confess your sin and put your trust in Christ to receive his full pardon.

Application for the believer; a call to respond to the gospel for the unbeliever.

Not Ashamed

Being called into ministry entails many tasks. We need to teach. We need to counsel. We need to minister to the poor, the sick, the dying. But one task rises above everything else: proclaiming the gospel. Without that, we can't build God's church. Paul wrote, "We preach Christ crucified: a stumbling block to Jews and foolishness to Gentiles, but to those whom God has called, both Jews and Greeks, Christ the power of God and the wisdom of God. For the foolishness of God is wiser than human wisdom, and the weakness of God is stronger than human strength" (1 Cor. 1:23–25). Why would we ever want to preach anything else? Yes, it's unfashionable in our culture. Yes, some people will be offended with the claims of Christ. Others might laugh at us. But Paul said, "I am not ashamed of the gospel, because it is the power of God that brings salvation to everyone who believes: first to the Jew, then to the Gentile" (Rom. 1:16).

May we never be ashamed of this message.

CHAPTER 5

The Unabridged Bible

*You know that I have not hesitated to preach
anything that would be helpful to you but
have taught you publicly and from house to
house. . . . I declare to you today that I am
innocent of the blood of any of you. For I have
not hesitated to proclaim to you the whole will
of God.*

—ACTS 20:20, 26–27

The first words God spoke, as recorded in Holy Scripture, were, "Let there be light" (Gen. 1:3). These words began the powerful transformation of the dark, formless wasteland called earth (Gen. 1:2) into something that earned the Creator's approval as being "very good" (Gen. 1:31).

The first words of Satan found in the Bible are not a statement, but rather a cunning question posed to the first woman: "Did God really say . . . ?" (Gen. 3:1). Eve and her husband had been placed in a perfect world, but with one restriction: "You must not eat fruit from the tree that is in the middle of the garden, and you must not touch it, or you will die" (Gen. 3:3). Satan's

73

first strategy was to question whether that command and promise really came from the Almighty and had his authority behind it.

Satanic attacks against the authority and importance of God's word continued throughout both the Old and New Testament eras. These assaults have increased exponentially in the twenty-first century. The surrounding culture goes far beyond questioning the authority of Scripture and brazenly maintains, as Satan did in the garden, "You will not certainly die" (Gen. 3:4). In other words, there is no divine law of sin and judgment. It also maintains that God and morality only restrict people from enjoying life and fulfilling their ultimate destiny of being "like God" (Gen. 3:5). "You and your desires should be at the center of everything" is the suggestion, not some invisible entity who wants to spoil your fun.

That the world of unbelievers is permeated with such thinking should come as no surprise to anyone. Satan is called "the god of this world" for good reason. But how those calling themselves Christians view the Word of God is another matter. If the Bible is not the authoritative source for our faith and practical living, we have no sure foundation. When the personal opinions of leaders and churchgoers win out over Scripture, we are in deep trouble whether we admit it or not. Jesus said, "Heaven and earth will pass away, but my words will never pass away" (Matt. 24:35).

Let's not forget that God is immutable. Through the prophet Isaiah, God once and for all established those with whom he is pleased: "These are the ones I look on with favor: those who are humble and contrite in spirit, and *who tremble at my word*" (Isa. 66:2). In too many church circles today, our cavalier attitude about the authority of all of Scripture has made it difficult to ascertain who's really in charge—us or God.

Let me show you what this looks like on the ground.

■ ■ ■

"I need your help with something."

My wife, Carol, was standing in the doorway to my office.

"I'm interviewing a young woman who wants to join the choir. She was in the worship group in her previous church and has an off-the-charts voice. But there's a problem."

As we walked down the hall, Carol told me what was going on.

Some background: When someone wants to join the choir in our church, they go through an interview process. They have to audition vocally, of course, so Carol can hear their voice and consider whether and how it might fit in. But they also have to be a member or plan to become a member of our church. Why? Because they need to be spiritually related with people who are over them in the Lord and might exercise spiritual authority over them when it's appropriate. Also, we want to make sure they understand the responsibility of publicly representing Christ as they sing.

I walked into Carol's office and saw a young woman seated there. I'll call her Cindy. I sat down across from her. "Cindy, Carol tells me there's a problem," I said.

She looked at me quizzically.

"What problem?"

"Carol tells me that you're living with your boyfriend. Is that true?"

She nodded.

I said, "Don't you see a problem with that in terms of the Word of God?"

She didn't. "We'll probably get married someday," she said. "But we love each other, and we're happy, so . . ."

We've all heard this logic before, haven't we? "God loves me. God wants me to be happy. What I'm doing makes me happy. So God must approve. Right?" Wrong. After a few minutes of sharing Scripture with her, I drew my chair closer. "Cindy, let me tell you what I'm going to do. I'm going to fight for you as if you were my own daughter." In addition to other Scriptures, I pointed out to her the list of "the acts of the flesh" in Galatians 5, starting with "sexual immorality, impurity and debauchery," and then Paul's summation: "I warn you, as I did before, that those who live like this will not inherit the kingdom of God" (Gal. 5:19, 21).

She started to cry. "Does this mean I can't join the choir?" she said.

"The *choir*? Cindy, it's not about the choir. Don't you understand what we're talking about here? You know what *repent* means, right? You're heading in one direction, and you need to make a 180-degree turn and go the other way. You can't go two ways at once. You can't have Jesus as Savior if you're living in the sin he died for." She grew silent.

"Listen," I finally said. "Give me your boyfriend's phone number, and I'll call him. Or here's my private office line. Have him call me. I'll talk to him. And we'll try to help you. We'll find you a place to stay. If you and your boyfriend get right before the Lord and the two of you want to get married, we'll be happy to help you. But we're going to have to walk through this carefully and make sure everything is right in God's sight."

She broke down and wept, but she chose to remain in her living situation. Even though she took my number, her boyfriend never called me. And we never saw Cindy again.

"I Never Held Back"

When Paul spoke to the elders in Ephesus, he knew it would be the last time he would speak to them. He wanted to strengthen their resolve for the task he knew lay ahead of them. One of those tasks would be preaching and teaching messages that the people might not want to hear. He cited his own example as a model for them to follow. "You know that I have not hesitated to preach *any-thing* that would be helpful to you but have taught you publicly and from house to house. . . . I have not hesitated to proclaim to you the *whole will of God*" (Acts 20:20, 27).

Notice that twice he used the phrase *I have not hesitated*. He was saying, "I never held back. I never avoided the inconvenient truths." He proclaimed the *whole* will of God to them, including the confrontational parts. He said he did this not only "public-ly"—to the entire congregation—but also "from house to house," or person-to-person. The introductory words *you know* sharpen this point a bit. It was important to him to be able to say, "You all know perfectly well that I never held back from preaching what I knew you needed to hear, even when it wasn't what you wanted to hear."

How about us? How ready are we to proclaim the *whole* will of God? Not only the words people *want* to hear but also the ones they *need* to hear? Do we teach not only what the Bible says about heaven but also what it says about hell? Not only the promises in Scripture but also the warnings? Not only about forgiveness but also about repentance?

I've spoken to pastors who have told me, matter-of-factly, "Listen, Jim, in my church, we don't talk much about sin. People don't come to church to hear negativity. They don't need to hear what's wrong in their lives." In other words, they don't want to confront people about their lifestyles because it might lower their attendance numbers. But let's be clear: God doesn't track our attendance records. He looks at the integrity of our teaching and the spiritual health of our people. That means he's interested in the kind of food we feed the sheep. He watches how and what we preach. We need to ask ourselves, Do we want people to grow in the Lord, or do we simply want them to come back next Sunday? Are we trying to please people, or are we trying to please God?

The Bible is our only guide. And if it's in God's Word, it must be important to preach about. For us leaders, this includes Paul's strong statement to the Ephesian elders that "I am innocent of the blood of any of you" (Acts 20:26). His declaration reminds me of God's word to the prophet Ezekiel:

> Son of man, I have made you a watchman for the people of Israel; so hear the word I speak and give them warning from me. When I say to the wicked, "You wicked person, you will surely die," and you do not speak out to dissuade them from their ways, that wicked person will die for their sin, and I will hold you accountable for their blood. But if you do warn the wicked person to turn from their ways and they do not do so, they will die for their sin, though you yourself will be saved. (Ezek. 33:7–9)

Likewise, Paul recognized the awesome responsibility that comes with preaching the gospel because of the enormously high stakes it involves. As he wrote to the Corinthians, "We are to God the pleasing aroma of Christ among those who are being saved and those who are perishing. To the one we are an aroma that brings death; to the other, an aroma that brings life. And who is equal to such a task?" (2 Cor. 2:15–16).

Who indeed? This is why the shallowness of much of the American pulpit today is frightening. I've visited churches where the service felt more like a late-night talk show. In fact, I was recently told of a preacher who boasted that he sharpened his "preaching skills" by listening to comedians and studying their timing. Imagine that! While our congregants struggle daily against "the powers of this dark world and against the spiritual forces of evil in the heavenly realms" (Eph. 6:12), some ministers look to comics as they focus more on a slick delivery than on the message itself! Can you picture Paul saying, "I've got to get to Rome and hear this new popular comedian"? As they say, you can't make this stuff up. What are people thinking?

Please don't think I'm an advocate for a "doom and gloom," legalistic, unloving style of ministry. That is not true Christianity. Our message, like Paul's, should be "the good news of God's grace" (Acts 20:24). When I was in college, God was beginning to deal with my heart in a deeper way, and I had a conversation with a wise, elderly pastor. He was reflecting on decades spent in the ministry. At one point, to my surprise, his eyes filled with tears. "For too many years, Jim," he said, "I gave the people ninety percent law and ten percent Jesus. I can't tell you how much I regret it." I've never forgotten his words.

While our message has to be about salvation through faith alone and not through obedience to the law, we also have to warn people about the wages of sin. How could we not, when Jesus said, "I have not come to call the righteous, but sinners to repentance" (Luke 5:32)? That was a summary of his calling. We have to proclaim that God's grace provides pardon for sins that are confessed to God: "If we confess our sins, he is faithful and just and will forgive us our sins and purify us from all unrighteousness" (1 John 1:9). That is not harsh or unkind. Remember that it was Jesus, the very embodiment of love, who warned, "What good is it for someone to gain the whole world, yet forfeit their soul?" (Mark 8:36).

Preach the Word

A word needs to be said here on the importance of the Bible in our preaching. Even if we're sincere and fervent, we must be rightly dividing the Word of God, which is our sole authority. As Samuel Chadwick said, "Passion does not compensate for ignorance."[1]

It's a terrible trend that more and more of the sermons being preached today aren't based on the Scriptures. This is contrary to what the apostle Paul urged Timothy to do: "Preach the word" (2 Tim. 4:2). Paul didn't tell Timothy to talk about visions or give his congregation his opinion on contemporary trends or politics. He didn't tell him to engage his audience in positive thinking or to appeal to their emotions. Paul knew that none of that would result in people growing in their faith. He knew that "faith comes by hearing, and hearing by the word of God" (Rom. 10:17 NKJV). We hinder people from growing in faith when we don't preach God's Word.

This lack of adherence to the Scriptures in our preaching may be partly to blame for the growing biblical illiteracy in our country; and sadly, it becomes a vicious cycle. The minister may be reluctant to base their sermon solely on the Bible if they feel the people aren't interested. But the less the people hear the Word, the less they know about the Word, and consequently, the less they *want* to hear the Word. This, in turn, causes preachers to focus even less on the Bible. But the biblical command is clear: Preach the word!

Christ's Ambassadors

Paul told the Corinthians, "We are therefore Christ's ambassadors, as though God were making his appeal through us" (2 Cor. 5:20). In that day, an ambassador was basically a mouthpiece. The ambassador was called before the king, received the king's message, and was sent out to deliver it. Not some of it, but all of it. Not his opinion of the message, just the message itself. Likewise, we must prayerfully deliver the Word of God, trusting the Holy Spirit to help us, even if opposition arises.

I experienced some of this opposition at a prayer conference I was invited to speak at several years ago. In the course of my message about King Asa, the subject of repentance of sin came up. I was saying that Asa's story reminds us that the Lord is with us when we are "with him" (2 Chron. 15:1–2), when we trust him and want to please him. But if we're living wrong and purposely disobeying his Word, he is saddened, and we won't experience his blessings.

Suddenly, the audience seemed to grow resistant. I could almost feel the tension in the air, the silent opposition. I thought, "Maybe I'm explaining it wrong." So I tried again. "What I'm saying is that the Lord is with us when we're with him. We have to be in agreement with his Word."

Now the tension became palpable. I took a deep breath. "Listen, folks," I said. "I didn't come here all the way from New York to tell you what you might want to hear. I came to preach God's Word as honestly as I can." The room was utterly silent. Then a man in the back, out of nowhere, yelled out with emotion, "Don't stop! Tell us. We need to hear it." I felt like that was the Lord's way of confirming that I was on the right track, so I pressed on. "Please listen to me," I said. "If we're living or acting contrary to God's Word, if we're cheating, stealing, hating, sleeping around, whatever it might be, how can we expect to experience Christ and his blessing? We're here to talk about prayer. But if we have iniquity in our hearts, the Lord won't hear our prayer until we repent and get right with him." Remember what the psalmist said: "If I had cherished sin in my heart, the Lord would not have listened" (Ps. 66:18).

That message was a struggle to the end. When I finished, I was sweating as if I had played full-court basketball for two hours. When I got back to my hotel room, I asked the Lord, "What was that all about? Did I get it wrong? Should I have even come to this place?" And I sensed the Lord speak to my heart: "You're here because I wanted you to be here, because I wanted those people to hear that message." We all appreciate affirmation from the audience when we preach. And sometimes that happens. Sometimes it doesn't. But we always have to remember that, ultimately, we have an audience of One. If we know we've given the message the Lord wanted us to give, that's all that matters.

Wise Parents, Good Physicians

I'm sure that when you were a child, you didn't always like the food your mother and father served you. It was the same for me. But our parents knew better than we did at our young age about our need for good nutrition if we were going to grow up strong and healthy. An interesting thing happened to me, and it was probably your experience as well. In time, I learned for myself what was nutritious and what wasn't. I even developed a taste for food that I didn't care for as a kid.

Our job as pastors is to feed the flock. But we do this as parents, not as servers in a restaurant. We don't hand them a menu and ask what they feel like having today. It's a dangerous day when the congregation determines the content and tone of the preaching. We need to feed the sheep good food if we want them to grow strong in the Lord—not just what they like, but what they need. And do you know what? If we do it in the right way, the Holy Spirit will confirm our words, and folks will grow spiritually stronger.

Here's yet another way to think about it. We sometimes call Jesus the Great Physician. When he was challenged about spending his time with sinners and tax collectors, he said, "It is not the healthy who need a doctor, but the sick. I have not come to call the righteous, but sinners" (Mark 2:17). Our role as ministers of Christ is to act as good doctors. Now think about what any good doctor does. They often give a variety of tests and then come back to us with the results. "Your blood pressure is dangerously high, and so is your cholesterol. You need to lose fifteen pounds, start an exercise regimen, and watch what you eat." How insane would it be for the patient to say, "Hey, doc! I didn't come here for negative thoughts about my health. Keep it positive. Just prescribe some of those red pills and a few white ones, and I'll be good to go." Doctors take the Hippocratic oath that binds them to the task of helping us get well, not telling us what we want to hear. So it is with pastors and church leaders as we follow in the steps of Jesus, the Great Physician.

Sharing the full gospel calls for courage. It also calls for wisdom and compassion. We need to be bold as lions and tender as lambs. Was Jesus bold? When he saw the money changers defiling the temple in Jerusalem, "he made a whip out of cords, and drove all from the temple courts, both sheep and cattle; he scattered the coins of the money changers and overturned their tables" (John 2:15). He once confronted the Pharisees with these words: "You brood of vipers, how can you who are evil say anything good?" (Matt. 12:34). That sounds rather bold to me.

But Jesus was also tender. He once said, "Come to me, all you who are weary and burdened, and I will give you rest. Take my yoke upon you and learn from me, for I am gentle and humble in heart, and you will find rest for your souls. For my yoke is easy and my burden is light" (Matt. 11:28–30). Who should come to him? All. Everyone who is burdened and needing rest. All ages, all races, all ethnicities. The Savior's love extends to all who heard him.

Admonitions and Warnings

It's admirable to want to comfort and encourage the flock. As shepherds, it's what we're called to do. But God's Word also has warnings about what following Christ means, and we must include these admonitions in our messages. Sugarcoating the facts about the Christian life helps no one and diminishes us as ministers.

Let's look at the words of Jesus to the church in Smyrna: "I know your afflictions and your poverty—yet you are rich! I know about the slander of those who say they are Jews and are not, but are a synagogue of Satan. Do not be afraid of what you are about to suffer. I tell you, the devil will put some of you in prison to test you, and you will suffer persecution for ten days. Be faithful, even to the point of death, and I will give you life as your victor's crown" (Rev. 2:9–10).

Jesus exhibited a frankness that many pastors would shy away from for fear that someone would say, "Hey, I'm not signing up for that!" Jesus didn't promise the believers in Smyrna a comfortable life. No, for them following Christ would include slander, per-secution, prison, and possibly even death! Opposition from the culture has varied throughout the centuries. Sometimes it has been subtle, at other times overt. But it will never disappear. As Jesus said, "If the world hates you, keep in mind that it hated me first. If you belonged to the world, it would love you as its own. As it is, you do not belong to the world, but I have chosen you out of the world. That is why the world hates you. Remember what I told you: 'A servant is not greater than his master.' If they persecuted me, they will persecute you also. If they obeyed my teaching, they will obey yours also" (John 15:18–20).

Down through history, believers in Jesus have at times suffered undeniable hardships. But it is by remaining faithful through such trials—even to the point of death—that we will likewise receive the victor's crown.

We need this reminder for the times in which we live. God has permitted a shaking during the COVID pandemic to discover the branches that are truly connected to Jesus Christ. American culture is also growing more hostile to the Christian faith at an alarming rate. The media, local and national governments, and the educational system are all increasingly anti-Christian and anti-Bible. And I believe this is just the beginning of an all-out assault against those who truly follow Jesus. The days ahead will not be easy. We will have to walk through a dark, hateful atmosphere to reach home. But this we can be sure of—as with the church in Smyrna, nothing ahead will surprise our heavenly Father, and nothing will cut us off from the love that Jesus has for us:

Who shall separate us from the love of Christ? Shall trouble or hardship or persecution or famine or nakedness or danger or sword? As it is written:

"For your sake we face death all day long;
we are considered as sheep to be slaughtered."
(Rom. 8:35–36)

Prophetic Fearlessness

The problem with the "feel-good" American gospel is not so much that its preachers don't use Scripture. The problem is that they cherry-pick a handful of verses that can be twisted to support their position. All the while, they purposely ignore the many verses that present a more sobering and realistic picture.

Let's not follow their example. Let's feed people good food so they'll grow. Let's not badger them, but let's also stay true to Scripture. Let's be like Paul, who said, "I have not hesitated to preach anything that would be helpful to you" (Acts 20:20).

And let's not be driven by the fear of losing people from our churches. If folks are unwilling to accept all of God's Word, we may need to ask whether they were ever really believers in the first place. We need courage to tell people everything that is needful and not avoid some topics for fear of a negative reaction. What's needed is a bold, fearless approach to preaching the whole counsel of God.

Imagine the horror of being responsible for someone spending eternity away from God. That person might say, "Why did you lie to me? I wake up in eternity and find I'm in a place of punishment. You never warned me that the wages of sin is eternal death." What do you say in response? "I didn't want to offend you"? "I didn't want you to leave my church"?

We have the privilege of feeding people the pure Word of God. We must do it boldly. One day they will see us in heaven and say, "Thank you for preaching Jesus and the true gospel. Thank you for giving it to me straight."

Here's what we need to remember: the Holy Spirit watches carefully how we treat the book he himself wrote. I fear that in many places, ignoring or twisting the Scriptures has driven the Holy Spirit from the very places where he longs to dwell. As we honor the Word of God and lift up Jesus Christ as the only Savior from sin, the Holy Spirit will empower us in ways we never knew possible.

The truth is that the Holy Spirit fire that we need to see ignited in our churches cannot burn brightly apart from the Word inspired by that same Spirit. A so-called revival that doesn't feed on God's pure Word will be characterized by shallow emotionalism and, ultimately, utter foolishness. Let's ask God today for a fresh movement of the Holy Spirit as we live daily on *every* word that proceeds from the mouth of the Father.

CHAPTER 6

WHO'S IN CHARGE HERE?

And now, compelled by the Spirit, I am going
to Jerusalem, not knowing what will happen
to me there. I only know that in every city the
Holy Spirit warns me that prison and hardships
are facing me.

—ACTS 20:22-23

In Acts 20:22–23 we have Paul's first mention of the Holy Spirit in his farewell address to the Ephesian elders. When I was growing up, I didn't have a good understanding of the Holy Spirit. (That people frequently spoke of the "Holy Ghost" in those days didn't help much.) As a child, I pictured the Spirit as a gas or a vapor. In other words, I thought of the Holy Spirit as an "it," not as a "he." But the Holy Spirit is a *person*, not a thing. This detail is more than semantics. It's crucial to understanding our relationship with the Spirit and the way he works in us and through us. Notice how many times Jesus refers to the Holy Spirit as "he" or "him":

Unless I go away, the Advocate will not come to you; but if
I go, I will send him to you. When he comes, he will prove

the world to be in the wrong about sin and righteousness and judgment. . . .

But when he, the Spirit of truth, comes, he will guide you into all the truth. He will not speak on his own; he will speak only what he hears, and he will tell you what is yet to come. He will glorify me because it is from me that he will receive what he will make known to you. All that belongs to the Father is mine. That is why I said the Spirit will receive from me what he will make known to you. (John 16:7–8, 13–15)

We see mentioned here the Father, the Son, and the Spirit. That doesn't indicate three gods, but rather the one true God existing as Father, Son, and Holy Spirit, in the mystery of the Godhead.

Jesus made clear in this discourse that when he went away, he would put someone else in his place. That person is the Holy Spirit. Jesus placed the Holy Spirit over his church on earth. He alone was given the job of directing and conducting all matters pertaining to Christ's church. And not only "the church" in the broad sense. He was to oversee individual churches—yours and mine.

I wonder how many of us believe that the Holy Spirit is to be in charge. He is the One who was sent to direct the affairs of every Christian church. Not the pastor. Not the board. Not the congregation. If anyone else is the bottom line of our churches, we're misguided. Pastors, elders, and boards are all important. But they're not all-important. No matter their intelligence, creativity, or talent, they're supposed to humbly seek the mind of the Spirit because the Spirit knows everything and is over everything.

That includes every major decision a church faces, even what pastors should preach about. Most pastors today are doing a sermon series, usually of some book in the Bible. That's fine—if the Holy Spirit has led that decision. But it's not wise to simply imitate what others are doing. Some of the pastors most used by

God in church history never or rarely preached in a series format. And if we're led to do that kind of exposition, we must always be ready to halt or cancel the series should the all-knowing Spirit of God so lead. He alone knows the needs and weaknesses of our people and what satanic plans are being devised, and thus he can give us the appropriate word in each season. "Whoever has ears, let them hear what the Spirit says to the churches" is said seven times by Christ himself in the letters to the churches found in Revelation 2 and 3. We should prayerfully obey that command, since the Holy Spirit has not changed. He still speaks to those who have a listening heart.

Follow the Spirit

I was having lunch at a café on Long Island on a Monday when I saw it. Thumbing through the newspaper, I came across an article about an anti-Christian rampage in the town of Gojra, Pakistan. A young couple had recently gotten married there, and the congregation had showered them with confetti as they left the church. Someone started a rumor that the confetti had been made by shredding a copy of the Qur'an, the central religious text of Islam. It wasn't true, but the rumor spread like wildfire. A mob of as many as twenty thousand went on an eight-day rampage in Gojra. Six members of a Christian family were burned alive inside their own home. According to one report, the Pakistani police stood by and watched all this happen but did nothing to stop it. Many Christians in Gojra had gone into hiding, in fear for their lives.

I'd heard other stories about similar incidents, and they always deeply saddened me. But this one had an unusually strong impact. I kept thinking, "Those are my brothers and sisters in Christ. And they're suffering." I couldn't even imagine the sheer terror of what they must have been going through.

I felt the Holy Spirit stirring my heart, and I prayed right there where I sat. Then I started to weep. And I couldn't stop. I sat there praying, with tears running down my cheeks and my face turned to the wall because I was embarrassed to be seen by the other people in the café.

I eventually left, but I remained troubled the rest of the day. I'd never been to Pakistan. I didn't know these people. I didn't know anything about them except that they were fellow Christians and they needed help desperately.

The next day we had our Tuesday night prayer meeting at the church. Shortly after the service began, I stood up and said, "Brothers and sisters, I need to share with you something that has been heavy on my heart." I read them a portion of the newspaper article. "Please excuse the emotion," I said when I finished. "But God has placed a burden on my heart for those believers. We need to pray."

Over a thousand people were in the building that night. I asked them to stand and break into groups of three or four to pray. And they did. They lifted their voices and called on the Lord for people they would undoubtedly never meet here on earth but with whom they would share eternity in heaven one day. The congregation was earnest and passionate in their praying. You could have heard them a block away.

After a while, I asked everyone to be seated. Just then, I saw one of our leaders hurrying down the center aisle toward the plat-form. He was waving his arms to get my attention, but I couldn't make out what he was saying. As he came closer, I heard him yelling, "Wife! Wife!" When he got to me, he told me that there was a Pakistani woman sitting in the back who was a pastor's wife and that I needed to hear what she had to say. I asked him to bring her up. When the woman walked up on the platform, I turned off my mic and spoke to her.

"Have you been here before?"

"No, I'm visiting from Pakistan."

"You're from Pakistan?"

"Yes, my husband is a pastor there. And he and my father-in-law were some of the first Christians to go to Gojra to help the people there."

"What?"

"Yes, they are there right now!"

I was dumbstruck.

She told me she had never been in New York City before. Somehow, for some reason, she had walked into our prayer meeting that night. I introduced her to the congregation and told them who she was and where she was from. A loud gasp went up from the church. We were all awestruck at what the Lord was doing right before our eyes.

I decided that now was the time to take the offering. I told the people, "This offering is for our brothers and sisters in Pakistan." And the people gave generously. The next day I asked Steve, our CFO, to check out the woman's story. He vetted it and talked to her husband—the pastor in Pakistan who was helping the believers in Gojra. Everything checked out, and we sent the money to those persecuted Christians.

Do you think that was all a coincidence? A woman from Pakistan who had never been to New York City before walked into our prayer meeting and heard me read a newspaper story about the place where her husband was ministering at that very moment. God then had our entire congregation pray for a besieged congregation in Pakistan. And he led us to take an offering for those believers in need.

No mind has ever conceived what the Holy Spirit can do if we yield to him.

■ ■ ■

In his speech to the elders in Ephesus, Paul said, "And now, compelled by the Spirit, I am going to Jerusalem" (Acts 20:22). Paul doesn't say *how* the Spirit compelled him. Perhaps it was simply by speaking to Paul's heart. Perhaps it was through a word of prophecy or a message in tongues accompanied by an interpretation in a gathering of believers. However the message came, Paul's answer was simple. He would follow the Spirit wherever he led. The Holy Spirit was in charge. He told Paul to go. So he went. The Spirit had replaced the ascendant Christ as the director of spiritual affairs for his people.

In his gospel, Mark tells us that Jesus's first words to Simon and Andrew were, "Come, follow me" (Mark 1:17). When Jesus saw James and John, "he called them, and they . . . followed him" (Mark 1:20). They went to Capernaum, where Jesus delivered a demon-possessed man and healed many people. The next morning, Jesus got up early and went out to pray. When the disciples found him, he said, "Let us go somewhere else—to the nearby villages—so I can preach there also" (Mark 1:38).

There's a pattern here. Jesus called his disciples, and they followed him. Not just in some general sense, but in the real-life, everyday sense. He said, "Today we're going here," and they went. If you saw Andrew on a Monday and asked him, "Where are you going next?" his answer would be, "We don't know. When Jesus tells us where we're going, then we'll know." The apostle Paul had the same attitude as he spoke to the Ephesian elders: The Holy Spirit is leading me. He's telling me to go to Jerusalem. So I'm going to Jerusalem.

Notice that the same principle can apply in the opposite sense. At one point during his second missionary journey, Paul wanted to go into Asia to preach, but the Holy Spirit prevented him (Acts 16:6). Here's what happened next: "When they came to the border of Mysia, they tried to enter Bithynia, but the Spirit of Jesus would not allow them to. So they passed by Mysia and went down to Troas. During the night Paul had a vision of a man of Macedonia standing and begging him, 'Come over to Macedonia and help us.' After Paul had seen the vision, we got ready at once to leave for Macedonia, concluding that God had called us to preach the gospel to them" (Acts 16:7–10).

Notice that to be led to Macedonia by the Spirit, Paul had to be first forbidden to preach the gospel in Bithynia by the same Holy Spirit. The apostle had learned how to yield constantly to the Spirit's direction.

■ ■ ■

Earlier I told you the story of the Pakistani Christians under siege and how the Holy Spirit had made a way for us to help them. But the story didn't end there.

On Saturday night of the same week, Steve, our CFO, called me. He had just been talking to the minister from Pakistan, and the news was grim. The pastor told Steve that something had set off the Muslims again during their evening call to prayer. "He said they're shouting, 'Death to the Christians! Death to the Christians!' He's afraid of what might be coming." Steve and I agreed that we would both pray that night and that the next day we would ask the church to pray as well.

The next morning, I went to the church and prepared for our Sunday nine o'clock service. My associate pastors and I were in my office, along with some of our prayer band members—seven or eight church members who pray with us before the services and then stay together and pray for us during each service. We finished praying. I was on my way to the elevator when one of our volunteers who was answering our phones that day called out to me.

"Pastor Cymbala, there's a phone call for you."

"I can't take it now; the service is about to begin."

"Pastor, the call is from Pakistan."

I made a U-turn. The call came through to my phone. I answered. It was the Pakistani minister. There was terror in his voice.

I asked, "What's going on?"

"We are trapped on the roof of a house. I'm up here with other believers from our church. There is a mob in the square carrying torches. They are working themselves into a frenzy. They are screaming, 'Death to the Christians! Death to the Christians!'"

"Okay," I said. "Be strong, brother. I'm going into our Sunday service now. And we're going to pray."

I hung up the phone and went downstairs as fast as I could. The service had begun, and the congregation was singing. I walked directly to the pulpit and interrupted the meeting. For the benefit of those who had not been at the prayer meeting, I told them what had happened on Tuesday. I then told the congregation what was happening in Pakistan at that very moment. "We need to pray right now!" I said.

The Holy Spirit helped us, and we prayed fervently, our hearts united in prayer for our Pakistani brothers and sisters in Christ. We continued praying for several minutes. Then a sense of peace settled over everyone. We felt confident that God had heard our prayer.

On Monday, Steve called and told me that he had talked to the Pakistani pastor again. And I thought, "Thank God he's alive!"

"Is he okay?" I asked.

"He's fine. But you're not going to believe what happened."

Steve then related the story.

The Pakistani church members had been stranded on the

roof, clinging to one another. Shortly after the pastor called me, dark clouds formed in the sky. It got dark, almost as dark as it gets after the sun goes down. Then it began to rain torrentially. It rained so hard that the crowd scattered and ran to their homes. And that was that. The tension was broken, and the Christians were able to get down from the roof and return to their homes.

Even now, when I look back on it, the whole story amazes me. It was something that only the Lord through his Holy Spirit could have done.

Following in Faith

Paul told the leaders from Ephesus that he was going to Jerusalem "not knowing what will happen to me there" (Acts 20:22). To our modern minds, that's an unsettling thought: Setting off on a new venture with no idea of what will happen next. No plan, no agenda; simply awaiting direction every day, every hour, every minute as to what we are to do. No corporation runs that way. Boards of directors and senior management teams don't look to the future and say, "Well, I don't know. Let's just go with the flow this year." Of course, Paul did make plans from time to time. But those plans were conditioned on the words *Lord willing.*

The bottom line is that Paul was ready to follow the Lord's direction, no matter what. How different from what we see today! The church has married the world, hailing its ideas as being all-wise and its methods all-powerful. And so the church has made what amounts to unholy spiritual alliances and treaties, following the world's latest fads and adopting its business models. Churches now boast more in their carefully developed one-year and even five-year plans than in the Holy Spirit's guidance.

It would do us well to remember the warning in Isaiah 30:1–3:

"Woe to the obstinate children,"
> declares the LORD,
"to those who carry out plans that are not mine,
> forming an alliance, but not by my Spirit,
> heaping sin upon sin;
who go down to Egypt
> without consulting me;
who look for help to Pharaoh's protection,
> to Egypt's shade for refuge.
But Pharaoh's protection will be to your shame,
> Egypt's shade will bring you disgrace."

God had delivered his people from Egypt. They were never to go back under any circumstances. Help from Egypt looked like a great blessing for beleaguered Israel. In the end, it brought disgrace.

We must ask ourselves two questions when analyzing approaches to ministry. First, where is the spiritual fruit that lasts the test of time? Jesus never planned for his church to be a revolving door, with commitment and consecration almost unknown.

Also, where are the testimonies of dramatically changed lives through the power of the gospel? The wild, uncontrollable demon-possessed man who met Jesus ended up sitting peacefully in his right mind (Mark 5:15). What a testimony of the power of the name of Jesus. Accepting Christ as Savior has always produced these true stories of "if anyone is in Christ, he is a new creation" (2 Cor. 5:17 NKJV). Old lifestyles of sin are altered and powerful addictions are broken only through Christ. We all want to show the world these kinds of "I was blind but now I see" testimonies. But there is a lack of such stories being told today in our churches. It's not because Christ has lost his power. Gospel preaching will likewise *always* produce changed lives.

Ministry that majors in clever sound and lighting productions along with carefully scripted entertainment-style services has no history. From the Protestant Reformation in the sixteenth century and across the centuries of solid Bible teaching, heartfelt prayer, and spreading the gospel to those needing Christ, there are no heroes who followed such a philosophy of ministry. When we look at the lives of Luther and the Reformers; the Puritans of the 1600s; the powerful ministries of Wesley and Whitefield as they boldly preached the gospel; the Great Awakening in colonial America; the preaching of Finney, Moody, Spurgeon, and General Booth during the nineteenth century; and all the way up to the gospel proclamation of Billy Graham in the last century, not one ever practiced the kind of shallow, "Christianity-lite" approach to ministry that we have today.

There might have been imperfections in both the people and the events the Lord used in the past, but they make a much better paradigm for young men and women entering the ministry today. Even as the prophets reminded Israel to look back in their history as to what God had done, we would do well to remember the best days of the Christian church. And those outstanding men and women in church history were inspired themselves by looking back to the book of Acts and the exploits of Peter, Paul, and others. In many places, leaders have disconnected from that great heritage and are going down a path of their own choosing. And now we are experiencing the inevitable "sowing and reaping" principle in our own congregations and nation.

Even my eleven-year-old grandson, Levi, who was adopted from Ethiopia, saw through one of these disturbing trends some months ago. He and his family had accompanied Carol and me one Sunday when we visited a local church. We happened to be there on a day when the senior pastor was casting his vision for his church. The minister said that one of the keys to building a dynamic church was contemporary signage, attractive colors for the auditorium, and modern lighting effects! When Carol and I exited the church into the parking lot, my grandson tagged along. He surprised us when he said, "Papa, remember how you told me that I might go back to my village in Ethiopia someday and tell people about Jesus? Well, when I do, I want to talk to the local pastors about their signage, interior colors, and lighting." This eleven-year-old knew enough about God to discern how foolish it was to consider those superficial fixes to be keys to effective ministry. Unfortunately, this kind of thinking is becoming more prevalent every day in our churches.

In the past, the Spirit meant everything. Now some would have him be nothing.[1] I sometimes ask myself: If the apostles were to come to America today and look at our churches, what would be their reaction? I'm convinced they would be taken aback. They would no doubt ask, "Where is the Holy Spirit in all this? How can you possibly carry on without him?" Samuel Chadwick was right when he said, "The Christian religion is hopeless without the Holy Ghost."[2]

As I travel around the country and the world, I often find myself asking these same questions. My firm belief is that we would bear more spiritual fruit, experience more of God's power, and spread the gospel further if we had a greater dependence on the Holy Spirit.

The apostles and the leaders of the early church relied on the Spirit because they had no other choice. They were simple people, fishermen and tax collectors, with not a single PhD or MDiv among them. I believe that one reason Jesus chose them is precisely *because* they were simple and unlearned. They would have had no choice but to rely on the Helper he promised to send them.

And although Christ had left them, they were not without a teacher. As leaders, we often forget this. "As for you, the anointing you received from him remains in you, and you do not need anyone to teach you. But as his anointing teaches you about all things and as that anointing is real, not counterfeit—just as it has taught you, remain in him" (1 John 2:27). The believers in our churches can be taught daily by the very One who inspired the Scriptures they read. Holy Spirit revelation of the Word of God is the best school to be in.

The knowledge we gain when earning a degree is not a bad thing in itself, of course, but it has a way of working in reverse. As Edward Dennett, the Plymouth Brethren preacher from the 1800s, said, "When knowledge enters the head, it exalts me; when knowledge enters the heart, it humbles me."[3] It's true that the more we learn, the more self-confident we often feel about our own abilities. We can then become mechanical as we carry out our responsibilities in the ministry. We think to ourselves, "I've got this." And we become less reliant on the Spirit. We lose the childlike openness to his promptings and direction. The danger is this: it is entirely possible to "do church" without the Holy Spirit. In America today, we have fine-tuned various methodologies for doing precisely that. A. W. Tozer once suggested that if the Holy Spirit were withdrawn from the earth today, most churches would not even notice his absence.

Not only was Paul going to Jerusalem "not knowing what will happen to me there," but the Holy Spirit had warned him that "in every city . . . prison and hardships are facing me" (Acts 20:22–23). That raises the stakes quite a bit. Think of the faith and the consecration it requires to keep going in light of such forewarnings. All of us want to be Spirit-led. But we also want to control things, and that's where the problem lies. We have to see a plan. We don't like to set out on a venture unless we know how it will end. And we probably won't embark on a journey if it means hardship and prison. Many of us might even use those prospective situations as proof that God was *not* leading us. But Paul was so radically dedicated to doing God's will that even "prison and hardship" would not weaken the surrender of his own will. Only the Holy Spirit can bring us to that kind of submission to the Lord.

Holy Bedlam

It was the Sunday afternoon service—the third service of the day, and we still had a fourth service to come—and I was tired. I was seated on the platform, and Carol was leading the choir. A time of praise and worship had opened the service, and now the choir was ministering. Leadership, along with some members of our prayer band, had prayed before the meeting as usual that the Holy Spirit would lead and bless the service. I've always felt that if God could lead the Israelites through the desert for forty years, day by day, he can lead us through a Sunday service.

The choir finished the first song. There may have been another one prepared, but for whatever reason when the first song ended, Carol closed her eyes and raised her hands in silent worship. Some of the choir members also raised their hands and worshiped the Lord. Soon a few people in the congregation did the same. A steady chorus of praise developed, and before long there was something in the air, a beautiful chord of adoration to God all through the building.

Something unexpected yet God-inspired was happening. But I wasn't sure what to do. I prayed, "Lord, what are you doing? What's supposed to happen? What should I do right now?" I stood up and slowly walked to the pulpit amid this heavenly sound. I stood there with a deep sense of weakness. I said, "Lord, I have a microphone here. What do you want me to do? If I start a chorus, everyone will sing. If I tell everyone to sit down, they'll sit down. But I'm not moving until you show me what to do. I'm not going to change the course of the service unless you lead me. Speak to me, Lord. Show me what to do." I was determined not to quench the Spirit, as he was invisibly directing something that no one could manufacture. The moment was sacred.

Then I opened my eyes, and my attention was drawn to a woman, the wife of one of the pastors, in the front row. She was standing quietly, eyes closed, hands raised, and I felt the Holy Spirit say to me, "Hand her the microphone."

My initial reaction? *What? I can't do that. I've never done that before. What if she just hands the microphone back to me?*

I could feel the pressure in my chest. My heart started pounding. I felt I'd grieve the Holy Spirit if I didn't do what he said. Unnoticed by most of the people praising God, I walked to the end of the platform, down the steps, and went toward her. I reached out to tap her shoulder—I didn't want to startle her—but before I could, she opened her eyes, turned toward me, took the microphone out of my hand, and immediately spoke a word from the Lord. Call it prophesying if you'd like—not predicting anything but reemphasizing the truth of the song the choir had just sung. "No, I will never leave you. I will never forsake you. You might think I've forgotten you. I have never forgotten you. I know exactly who you are and where you are, and I will never abandon you." It wasn't a new revelation not already found in Scripture. But the weight and power of her words were indescribable.

In that moment, we had heaven visit earth. Without anyone uttering a word of invitation or instruction, the choir praised God and people stood—some came to the altar, others knelt down. No one on the platform had led what was happening, yet it was totally in order. I sat there in the front row, thinking, "I'd rather be here in God's manifest presence than any other place in the world."

Two days later the woman's husband came into my office. "Jim," he said, "that was an amazing afternoon service, right? God was certainly gracious in visiting us." I replied, "It was special. Times of refreshing do come from the presence of the Lord."

He told me that when he and his wife were driving home, he said to her, "God really used you in the service." She was quiet. He asked her, "But how in the world did you get the microphone from Pastor Jim?"

She said, "Well, I sensed a message in my heart, a word for the church, to encourage them. But I wasn't sure if it was really God. And I thought, my voice is so quiet, and the sound of praise is all around me. Even if I speak out, no one will hear me. So I said, 'God, if this is really you, make the pastor come down from the platform and hand me the microphone. Then I'll know it's from you.'"

Being led by the Spirit isn't always that dramatic. But it *is* always that important.

Filled with the Spirit

We've all heard, and probably used, the expression "filled with the Spirit." What does it mean? It may seem obvious. But let's dig a little deeper.

We all understand and agree that the Holy Spirit is a person. And we all understand and agree that all Christians have the Holy Spirit living inside them. "If anyone does not have the Spirit of Christ, they do not belong to Christ" (Rom. 8:9). But are all Christians "filled" with the Spirit? And are they "filled" once and for all?

It doesn't seem that way. On the day of Pentecost, the disciples prayed, and "all of them were filled with the Holy Spirit" (Acts 2:4). A short time later, when Peter and John were brought before the high priest and his family, Peter was "filled with the Holy Spirit" (Acts 4:8). Then when Peter and John were released after a night in prison, they returned to the believers and they all prayed. "After they prayed, the place where they were meeting was shaken. And they were all *filled with the Holy Spirit* and spoke the word of God boldly" (Acts 4:31).

But wait a minute. These were the same people who were together on the day of Pentecost (Acts 2:1–4). If they were all filled with the Spirit then, why did they need to be filled again?

Paul told the Christians in Ephesus to "be filled with the Spirit" (Eph. 5:18). The Greek literally means to "be being filled with the Spirit." It's what grammarians call the present continuous tense. At least one translation renders it "keep on being filled with the Spirit." If everyone was filled at one point, and if they remained filled from that point forward, why would Paul have to command them to keep on being filled?

Here's another example. When the apostles were addressing the problem of the distribution of food among the widows in the early church, they directed the church to "choose seven men from among you *who are known to be full of the Spirit* and wisdom" to take over the process (Acts 6:3). If *everyone* was already full of the Spirit, how could that serve as an indicator of who should be selected? Also, we know the church in Laodicea was a Christian church. But Spirit-filled? Apparently they were lukewarm, so Christ was about to spit them out of his mouth (Rev. 3:16).

The imagery of "being filled" makes sense if we are talking about a bucket filled with water or a tank filled with propane gas. Although such imagery as water, wind, and oil is used in Scripture, the Holy Spirit is none of these. He is a person. So what does it mean to be "filled" with a person?

Think about what it means when Scripture says that someone is demon possessed. It means that demonic spirits control and animate the person. To be filled with the Spirit also means to be controlled and quickened, but by the Holy Spirit, as a result of a fresh surrender to him. And with this fresh surrender comes a fresh impartation of power from Almighty God.

That's good news. It means that the more we continue to surrender ourselves to the Spirit, the more he can grant his power to us in new and different ways.

Deprived of the Spirit

While it's possible for us to experience new impartations of the Spirit's blessings, it's also possible to miss out on—or even to reject—the Holy Spirit's help. Scripture speaks of at least two ways this can happen. We can *grieve* the Spirit. And we can *quench* the Spirit.

To "grieve" the Holy Spirit means to disappoint him, to make him sad. How do we do that? One way is by failing to treat one another as the Lord wants us to. "Do not grieve the Holy Spirit of God, with whom you were sealed for the day of redemption. Get rid of all bitterness, rage and anger, brawling and slander, along with every form of malice. Be kind and compassionate to one another, forgiving each other, just as in Christ God forgave you" (Eph. 4:30–32).

Paul also wrote, "Do not quench the Spirit" (1 Thess. 5:19). Scripture often uses the metaphor of fire to describe the Spirit and his work in our midst. In Acts 2 the disciples "saw what seemed to be tongues of fire that separated and came to rest on each of them. All of them were filled with the Holy Spirit" (vv. 3–4). And remember that John the Baptist said Jesus would baptize "with the Holy Spirit and fire" (Matt. 3:11). The image Paul uses of quenching the Spirit is like someone pouring water on that fire. When we interrupt or interfere with the Spirit's work among us, when we belittle or neglect his important role, it's as if we literally pour water on the fire of the Spirit. My personal conviction is that untold numbers of Bible-believing, orthodox churches are silent opponents of the Holy Spirit. He is not welcomed to take charge among them. The order of service and the script can't be altered, even by God himself. And that is a tragedy. E. M. Bounds said the Holy Spirit must have freedom, or he will have nothing.

If the Holy Spirit is not in charge of the church of Jesus Christ on earth, we neglect him at our own peril. How are we to be guided in our decision-making or empowered for ministry without the Spirit? How are we to preach the gospel and make converts? Will talent, marketing programs, and cleverness lead people to repentance? It is the Holy Spirit, after all, who has come to convict the world of sin (John 16:8). How can we hope to come against the power of the devil without the power of the Holy Spirit? Paul warned the Ephesians to "be strong in the Lord and *in his mighty power*" (Eph. 6:10). We can intellectually understand the various parts of the armor of God (shield, helmet, and so on), but without the power of the Spirit, we can't live victoriously for Christ.

Balancing Word and Spirit

We live in a day when many people who love God and love Jesus and love their Bibles are somewhat leery of the Holy Spirit. Why? Because some Christian television programs have so much unbiblical fanaticism, and some churches attribute bizarre manifestations to the Holy Spirit. Serious Christians who know their Bible see such things and say, "This does not edify the church, and that includes me." And they're right. On that note, the presence of the Holy Spirit is neither a "vibe" nor an ethereal atmosphere created by music and a fog machine.

One of the most difficult tasks we face is finding the balance between Word and Spirit. It's important that we do find it, though, because going too far in either direction creates problems. I've often repeated something my friend Warren Wiersbe used to say: "If you emphasize only the Word, you dry up. If you emphasize only the Spirit, you blow up. If you emphasize *the Word and the Spirit*, you grow up." The Bible is our only rule of faith. But without the Spirit breathing on it and leading our services, everything soon will be only "north of the neck," with our hearts unmoved. Satan has played both ends against the middle in this regard, hasn't he? So we have to find the balance, combining loyalty to the Word with the prayer, "Come, Holy Spirit!"

How do we do this? Here's one benchmark. When the Holy Spirit comes, he doesn't draw attention to himself; he glorifies Christ. Satan's strategy is to counterfeit the true Holy Spirit and produce unhealthy emotionalism, unbiblical weirdness, and egotistical charlatans to give the Spirit a bad name. But we mustn't throw out the baby with the bathwater. If we truly adhere to Scripture, we shouldn't be closed to the idea of the Holy Spirit's gifts and manifestations. There's no reason not to hope, and even expect, that he'll do all the powerful things in our day that he did in the Bible. We shouldn't have any problem with the idea that God might heal people, deliver people, and bring thousands to salvation through a single sermon. He did it before. Why shouldn't he do it again? Why wouldn't we want him to? Why shouldn't we pray that he will? Our present-day circumstances in a world filled with darkness and despair should certainly cause us to cry out for help from heaven.

When it comes to a fresh openness to the Holy Spirit, we shouldn't be afraid that some satanic counterfeit will spoil things. We have God's sure Word to help us. The simple test of any manifestation of the Spirit is whether it serves to build up the people of God, to edify them. "Now to each one the manifestation of the Spirit is given for the *common* good" (1 Cor. 12:7). And later Paul said, "Everything must be done *so that the church may be built up*" (1 Cor. 14:26).

If an activity or a manifestation spiritually edifies the people of God, building up their faith, drawing them closer to Christ, getting them to love their Bibles more, then that's God at work. Would Satan or the flesh be producing such results? A tree is known by its fruit.

I recognize these are controversial subjects in some quarters. Some parts of the church have, in effect, branded themselves in terms of their disbelief in the Holy Spirit operating today. But shouldn't we seek all that the Holy Spirit has for us? He's the one who inspired the Scriptures, empowers us so we can work for our Lord, and produces the fruit that makes us daily more like Jesus. I've always loved the chorus of "Spirit of the Living God" that I first heard many years ago. I trust that its words will be a prayer we all can pray.

> *Spirit of the Living God,*
> *Fall fresh on me,*
> *Spirit of the Living God,*
> *Fall fresh on me.*
> *Break me, melt me, mold me, fill me.*
> *Spirit of the Living God,*
> *Fall fresh on me.*[4]

CHAPTER 7

PREACHING IN THE
POWER OF THE SPIRIT

My message and my preaching were not
with wise and persuasive words, but with a
demonstration of the Spirit's power.
–1 CORINTHIANS 2:4

Paul had spent three years preaching the gospel in Ephesus. He was now on his way to Jerusalem, where he knew other opportunities would arise to proclaim Christ. Before we go further, however, let's take a closer look at Paul's philosophy of preaching.

Paul's preaching was rooted in the truth of God's Word but accompanied by the power of the Spirit. In his first letter to the Corinthians, Paul described his preaching: "I did not come with eloquence or human wisdom as I proclaimed to you the testimony about God. For I resolved to know nothing while I was with you except Jesus Christ and him crucified. I came to you in weakness with great fear and trembling. My message and my preaching were not with wise and persuasive words, but with a demonstration of the Spirit's power, so that your faith might not rest on human wisdom, but on God's power" (1 Cor. 2:1–5).

"I did not come with eloquence or human wisdom" (1 Cor. 2:1). No Bible school or seminary I know of teaches this approach to preaching. Most teach precisely the opposite; the whole point is to help students sound scholarly, persuasive, clever—to make them great communicators. Paul boasts that his preaching wasn't like that. He wanted his followers' faith to rest not on his eloquence but on God's power. Paul didn't want to impress people as a great communicator; he wanted them to know the greatness of Jesus. Keep in mind the cultural context in which Paul made this statement. Greco-Roman culture revered wisdom and oratory. They idolized leading philosophers in the same way that we idolize superstar athletes and entertainers today. Paul wouldn't have any of that.

That's an important lesson for all of us. When members of your congregation go home on Sunday talking about the talent of the preacher or the worship team, that service somehow missed the mark. If they leave saying, "I encountered the living Christ today," the service was a success.

"I resolved to know nothing while I was with you except Jesus Christ and him crucified" (1 Cor. 2:2). Paul ministered with a laser focus on the crucified Christ. His subject matter was the virgin birth, the cross Jesus died on, his blood shed to atone for sin, his resurrection, the promise of the Holy Spirit, and the second coming of Christ. Paul's example is one we must follow if we want to preach in the power of the Spirit.

Jesus spoke about the Holy Spirit's ministry in these terms: "When the Advocate comes . . . he will testify about *me*" (John 15:26). He added later, *"He will glorify me* because it is from me that he will receive what he will make known to you" (John 16:14). The great mission of the Holy Spirit is to glorify Jesus.

Although he brings many other blessings, exalting Christ is his chief work. This is a vital fact to remember when we prepare our sermons and preach to people.

The Holy Spirit will help us as we glorify Jesus Christ, and no one else, in our messages. If the speaker uses the microphone to subtly draw attention to himself rather than Christ, the Spirit's help will be absent. The same goes for highlighting "how wonderful our church is" or "how special our denomination is compared to others." The Spirit will patiently wait on the side if we go down any rabbit holes of self-glorification. He was not sent to glorify you or me, our local church name, or any brand or denominational label. He came to exalt Jesus and Jesus only. When we are on the same page with the Holy Spirit, and in agreement with his mission, we will experience his help in amazing ways. Drawing attention away from Christ is one of the fastest ways to quench the Spirit.

It's hard to think of anything so directly at odds with our society's culture and values as the message of salvation through Christ. The culture extols athletes, billionaires, and entertainers. It recoils at the gospel message of a Savior named Jesus, who was beaten, spit upon, and nailed to a cross to atone for sin. But note this: that message was every bit as alien and distasteful to the culture Paul preached to. "We preach Christ crucified: a stumbling block to Jews and foolishness to Gentiles, but to those whom God has called, both Jews and Greeks, Christ the power of God and the wisdom of God" (1 Cor. 1:23–24). Paul didn't let the sensibilities of the surrounding culture stop him. We shouldn't let them stop us either. The only way that's going to happen is to be so taken up with God's approval that we're immune to the reaction of others.

"I came to you in weakness with great fear and trembling" *(1 Cor. 2:3).* Why was Paul fearful and trembling? I don't think it was stage fright. Paul was as bold and fearless a preacher as the

world has ever seen. I think it came from a deep concern that he would not preach Christ with perfect clarity, or that the Holy Spirit's power wouldn't accompany his message. We should share that same concern. God has sent us to deliver his gospel in the power of the Spirit. That must be our goal—not the applause our sermons might bring.

"My message and my preaching were not with wise and persuasive words, but with a demonstration of the Spirit's power" (1 Cor. 2:4). What was the "demonstration of the Spirit's power" that accompanied Paul's preaching? There's no hint that it was a constant manifestation of the gifts of the Spirit. Paul did perform miracles through the Spirit, but there are no miracles-upon-demand found anywhere in the New Testament.

What Paul did was deliver the good news about Jesus while relying on the Spirit to bring it home to the hearts of the people. Peter similarly relied on the Spirit in his ministry, as recorded in the book of Acts. In Acts 2, after Peter finished his sermon, the people "were cut to the heart and said to Peter and the other apostles, 'Brothers, what shall we do?'" (Acts 2:37). That wasn't because of Peter's oratorical skills. It was because the Holy Spirit applied the gospel to the listeners' hearts.

This marriage of the message and the vessel can be accomplished only through the Holy Spirit. As the Methodists of prior years maintained, "Evangelism becomes effective only through the power of the Spirit within the evangelist."[1]

Deep Conviction

A friend of mine named Charles once shared with me an interesting experience he had that illustrated the power of the Holy Spirit that is available to us. When Charles was in seminary, a guest lecturer gave a series of talks about preaching. About five minutes into the first session, Charles thought, "This is the most boring guy I've ever heard." The man's voice was utterly monotone. Charles struggled to keep his focus on the presentation. "But as he continued to speak," Charles said, "I felt as if my heart was being squeezed. I can't really describe the sensation. Then, suddenly, I felt like I was going to cry. Jesus and his love had become so real. I tried to hold back the tears, but eventually I couldn't do it. I continued to weep. I felt embarrassed. But then an odd thing happened. As we took a coffee break, I noticed everyone else in the group was also wiping away tears! It went on like that all week long. By any normal standard, the man was no great orator. But the Holy Spirit was with him. There was power in his words that gripped our hearts."

Here's another account by a noted preacher, describing the difference the Spirit makes in preaching:

> Oh, my brethren, when the Holy Spirit visits a man, what a difference it makes in him! I know a preacher, once as dull and dead a man as ever misused a pulpit. Under his slumbering ministry, there were few conversions, and the congregation grew thinner and thinner. Good men sighed in secret, and the enemy said, "Aha, so we would have it." Revival came, the Holy Spirit worked glorious, the preacher felt the divine fire and suddenly woke up to energy and zeal. The man appeared to be transformed; his tongue seemed to be touched with fire. Elaborate and written discourses were laid aside, and he began to speak from his own glowing heart to the hearts of others. He preached as he had never done before. The place filled, the dry bones were stirred, and a quickening began. The Spirit of God is a great wonderworker![2]

Who was the noted preacher relating this dramatic turnaround in another man's ministry? It was Charles Spurgeon, the famous Baptist pastor from London, England, who was called the Prince of Preachers. Spurgeon knew all too well the vital importance of the Holy Spirit *on* the preacher as they minister.

Paul elsewhere wrote something similar to this, but with an important addition: "Our gospel came to you not simply with words but also with power, with the Holy Spirit and *deep conviction*" (1 Thess. 1:5).

Paul suggested that a key to successful preaching is "deep conviction." The original Greek suggests that he was talking about deep conviction not in the hearer but in the speaker. And that makes sense. How can we affect others with God's truth if we ourselves aren't first convicted of it by the Holy Spirit? How can we preach, let's say, that love is patient (1 Cor. 13) unless God deals with us afresh about our own impatience? Unless God's Word goes deeper with us first, our messages likely won't have the ring of spiritual authority that they need. What we say may be true. It may be doctrinally sound. But unless it's said with deep conviction produced by the Holy Spirit, it won't penetrate the hearts of the people.

My biggest struggle when I first went into the ministry was believing God could use me despite my conversational way of speaking. I felt I needed to sound more "ministerial"—you know, with a more religious tone in my voice. I kept trying to remember how the pastors I had seen growing up carried themselves so I could imitate them and lessen my self-consciousness.

About four months into the ministry, Carol and I were driving home from church one morning, and I asked her, "How am I doing?"

"Do you really want to know?"

When your wife says that to you, you recognize immediately

that maybe you don't really *want* to know, but you definitely *need* to know.

"Yes. I really want to know. How am I doing?"

"Terrible."

"Okay. Why?"

"Because when you're preaching, you're not really *you*. You're playing a part. You're trying to act like a preacher."

She was right, of course. I was insecure. I didn't have faith that God could use me just the way I am. But God doesn't make any two snowflakes exactly alike, and it's the same with preachers. I don't need to imitate anyone else. That's the formula for spiritual failure. The world needs my voice, not an echo. God had to show me it's not how I speak that matters; it's how he works when I speak.

It's the Spirit who gives weight to our words. He lends an authority that we can't get by fine oratory, theatrical mannerisms, or a "tear in your voice." It's either there or it's not. Remember the account in Scripture of the two men walking to Emmaus when—though they did not recognize him—the risen Jesus came alongside and walked with them, explaining to them all the Scriptures concerning himself. Later they said to each other, "Were not our hearts *burning* within us while he talked with us on the road and opened the Scriptures to us?" (Luke 24:32). They never mentioned how clever or eloquent Jesus was, but only that their hearts were deeply stirred. That is probably the greatest need in church pulpits across America—preaching that produces burning hearts as Jesus did. May the Lord light that fire in each of our hearts!

Holy Spirit, Help Me!

Early in my ministry, I was invited to speak at a church in a poor part of South America during the heat of summer. I'm pretty sure the only reason I was invited was because my father-in-law knew the pastor and his wife. I arrived bright and early at the church, trying to look good in my blue seersucker suit.

I'd only just begun speaking when I got the uncomfortable sense that things weren't going well. I felt as if I were preaching to a wall. A high, gray, concrete wall. It was as if my words were bouncing off that wall and coming back at me. So I tried harder. Nothing happened. So I prayed. "God, I'm preaching, but they're not receiving. They're just sitting there, staring at me. Something is really wrong in this place." I became desperate. "Holy Spirit, please! *Help me!*"

As I was closing my message, I felt God direct my attention to a well-dressed lady sitting in the last row. I immediately called out to her: "Excuse me, ma'am—in the last row, with the blond hair—would you please come up here? I'd like to pray for you." She stood up and walked slowly to the front of the church. Why I was prompted to do that I wasn't exactly sure, and I didn't know what to do next.

It turned out I didn't need to do anything. The moment the woman reached the altar, she fell to her knees and began to sob softly. That was a little unexpected. Then other people came forward. That was even more unexpected. I hadn't made an "altar call," as it's called. But here they came. Five people. Ten people. Fifteen. Twenty. The pastor and his wife moved among them, praying with one, then another. The next thing I knew, people were weeping and hugging one another. I had no idea what was happening, but it went on for quite a while. I just stood there watching. I never did properly finish the sermon.

Later I had dinner at the pastor's home.

"Thanks for coming," he said.

"Well, I did my best," I replied. "I was really struggling there for a while."

He told me he knew exactly what I had experienced because

the church had been like that for several months. "There's been no blessing nor a sense of the Holy Spirit," he said. "It's like everything has come to a standstill. And we know the reason. We're experiencing terrible division in the church. People are whispering, spreading all kinds of gossip. And the source of it all was the woman you called forward. When she broke down the way she did, all the others who've been part of the division realized that God was not pleased and they'd better repent."

I had no inkling of any of this while preaching the sermon. Suddenly the Holy Spirit had come and worked in the hearts of the people, and the pastor saw a great reconciliation come about. My sermon certainly wasn't eloquent, but the Holy Spirit had dealt with a deep spiritual problem.

Praying As We Preach

My prayer that day—"Holy Spirit, *help me!*"—wasn't something I had carefully composed and rehearsed. It was spontaneous and from my heart. One might say it was a natural response to the predicament I found myself in. But I don't think it was only a natural response. I believe I had the supernatural assistance of the Holy Spirit as promised in Scripture: "The Spirit helps us in our weakness. We do not know what we ought to pray for, but the Spirit himself intercedes for us through wordless groans . . . the Spirit intercedes for God's people in accordance with the will of God" (Rom. 8:26–27).

Have you ever been in a situation where you were tired or confused and you couldn't even figure out how to pray or what to pray for? Christ gave the Holy Spirit to help us in those very situations. How few believers take that promise to heart! We struggle, we become mechanical in our prayers, when all along the Spirit is there to help us if we look to him.

In Paul's discourse on spiritual warfare, he directs us to take up the full armor of God, which includes the belt of truth, the breastplate of righteousness, the shield of faith, the helmet of salvation, and the sword of the Spirit. Paul then explains what makes all those weapons work effectively together: "And pray in the Spirit on all occasions with all kinds of prayers and requests" (Eph. 6:18). This was a common practice for the apostle—letting the Spirit inspire and empower his prayers. The Holy Spirit also imparts the fervency and faith needed for big prayer tasks.

Jude, our Lord's half-brother, adds that this kind of praying is essential if we're to keep strong until the return of Christ: "Dear friends, by building yourselves up in your most holy faith and *praying in the Holy Spirit*, keep yourselves in God's love as you wait for the mercy of our Lord Jesus Christ to bring you to eternal life" (Jude vv. 20–21).

The secret for receiving the Spirit's help is to admit that we are weak and open our hearts to him. Paul delights that he can pray with his understanding but also pray with his spirit, helped by the Holy Spirit who dwells within him (1 Cor. 14:15).

Because much of the body of Christ undervalues the Holy Spirit, praying in the Spirit has been wrongly relegated to only the first-century church. But Paul's words constitute good advice for Christians today as well. It's particularly good advice for pastors, who need the Spirit's help with preaching and counseling, along with confronting obstacles and opposition. If the great apostle Paul was thankful for the blessing of prayer "in the Spirit," wouldn't it also benefit you and me?

We should always pray for God's help prior to preaching his Word. But the Holy Spirit can also work *while* we preach. We have to look to him in the moment, right then and there. We have to learn to preach to people while our hearts wait in faith for God's assistance. Remember, we can never put the Spirit in a box. The Wind blows whenever and wherever he wants.

All this is especially true if we preach a message we've preached before that has received a good response. Then we might think, "I'm good. This sermon works." But the reality is that nothing "works" but God. No sermon. No song. Nothing. We may be able to stir surface emotions, but no deep work in people's lives is possible except with the Spirit's help.

I've learned that my ministry helps more people when I'm conscious of my need of the Holy Spirit as I'm speaking. We of course focus on those listening to us, since we want to bless them with God's truth. But it's even more important to be aware of God's presence. His anointing imparts the power and wisdom we need to preach in a way that gains God's approval. The last thing in the world Isaiah, Jeremiah, or John the Baptist thought about was getting applause. They only wanted to please the One who sent them.

Prophetic Preaching

In that vein, one of the great needs in the church today is to recapture the prophetic element in preaching. By that I don't mean *foretelling*—predicting future events—but rather *forthtelling*. Part of the prophets' role—perhaps the main part—was to proclaim what God wanted to say to a particular group of people at a particular time; that is, not so much what will occur in the future but what God feels about what is happening now.

I often hear people ask the question, "What is God saying to the church?" In Revelation chapters 2 and 3, we find a series of letters from Jesus to churches in various cities. Each of the seven letters ends with the same words: "Whoever has ears, let them hear what the Spirit says to the churches" (Rev. 2:7). What is God saying to the church? Well, it all depends on which church you're in. The letter to the church in Ephesus couldn't be transferred to the church in Smyrna or Pergamum or Thyatira because Jesus was saying different things to each of them.

For those of us who are pastors, the important question to ask is, "What is the living Holy Spirit saying to *my* church today?" If Jesus were here on earth, what would he say this Sunday morning to my church or yours? Where are we weak? What is the spiritual temperature of the congregation? What words of encouragement or correction would he give? The noted revivalist Charles G. Finney suggested that one path to finding that out is to live among our people and get to know them better. Find out where they're hurting, where they're being deceived by Satan, what sins they're excusing or rationalizing. Then we need to get alone with God and his Word until the Holy Spirit gives us the right message.

It's noteworthy that the first sermon of the Christian era took place after a prayer meeting. The disciples were "all together in one place" (Acts 2:1) when the Holy Spirit came upon them. As they loudly spoke in "tongues" (languages they did not know), it drew a crowd (Acts 2:4–6). Those people became the audience for the apostle Peter's sermon (Acts 2:14–40). (By the way, Peter used no notes, nor did he even anticipate preaching that day!) That sermon was important, to be sure. But it was protracted prayer, not preaching alone, that gave birth to the Christian church. The importance of prayer in ministry was affirmed hundreds of years later by Andrew Bonar, leader of the Scottish revival, when he said, "I have learned by experience that it is not much labor but much prayer that is the only means to success."[3]

This emphasis on prayer is aligned with Paul's priorities. He instructed Timothy, "I urge, then, *first of all*, that petitions, prayers, intercession and thanksgiving be made for all people—for kings and all those in authority, that we may live peaceful and quiet lives in all godliness and holiness. . . . Therefore I want the men everywhere to pray, lifting up holy hands without anger or disputing" (1 Tim. 2:1–2, 8).

Note the words *first of all*. Prayer was Paul's first priority for the church.

It's also interesting that the disciples never said to Jesus, "Lord, teach us to preach," or, "Lord, teach us how to do church." Rather, they said, "Lord, teach us to pray" (Luke 11:1). They had seen Jesus getting up early in the morning, sometimes staying up all night, going off by himself to talk with his Father and wait in his presence. They knew that was the secret of his powerful ministry and spiritual authority; and they wanted to learn how to pray as he did.

Today, preachers can use computer software and commentaries to help polish their sermons. Or worse, they can steal sermons from others. But the sermon is supposed to be only an arrow that points people to God. We've too often made the sermon the end-all of Christian ministry, but it's not. *God* is! And how can we see people drawn to a new fellowship with God if we aren't spending time alone with him ourselves? Prayer is the highest form of communion with God here on earth. It is in prayer that we "approach God's throne of grace with confidence, so that we may receive mercy and find grace to help us in our time of need" (Heb. 4:16).

"Lead My People to Pray"

Carol and I had been at the Brooklyn Tabernacle about two years, struggling with a small congregation, meager offerings, and a neighborhood riddled with alcohol, heroin, and gang violence.

One day, while both discouraged and bewildered, I sensed the Lord make me a threefold promise. He said that if we would lead the people to pray, he would provide me with all the sermons I would ever need; that he would supply all the money we would ever need, both personally and for the church; and that there would never be a building large enough to contain in a single service all the people he would send our way. He would do all these things *if* we would lead the people to pray.

So I focused on the church's Tuesday night prayer meeting. The first night we met, I think there were about twelve people in our tiny auditorium. It grew from there—slowly, but it grew. Over the years it became the foundation of our church, the engine that drives everything we do. And God has fulfilled every promise he made to me.

Some years later, one of our associate pastors came to me and said, "Pastor, I see you preaching and pouring yourself out on Sundays. Would you mind if I gather some people who will pray during the services? We'll ask God to help you, anoint the choir, and bless the meeting." Who could say no to that? That was the beginning of our church's prayer band. We now have several hundred people who are committed to praying from morning to evening in our building, in shifts of several hours each, not only for me or the church but also for requests that come in from all over the world.

I recently got a telephone call from a confused associate pastor in another state who had a different experience. He'd gone to his senior pastor to ask if they might start a weekly prayer meeting or at least include more prayer in the Sunday services. The senior pastor replied, "Sorry, that's not my vision for us. It's not the model we're following." I've heard more stories like that than I care to remember. Not our model? How can we have a model different than the one Jesus gave *his* own church? If what we're doing is not centered in communion with God, what book are we reading? Of course, we can try anything we want, but it will lack God's blessing and bear little fruit in the end.

Didn't Jesus say that his father's house was to be called a house of prayer? Do we not want our churches to be houses of prayer and not just houses of preaching or Bible study? All those things are important. But not more important than the kind of prayer Paul instructed Timothy to lead the people into: "petitions, prayers, intercession and thanksgiving . . . for all people—for kings and all those in authority" (1 Tim. 2:1–2). Aren't there enough situations around us that need God's intervention? Backslidden church members? Marriages in decay? Wayward children? People who are sick? On drugs? In financial need? How can we say prayer isn't part of our model? Too many leaders lack faith in God's explicit promises about prayer, so they end up merely following some trendy model or trying to replicate some denominational tradition. But God hasn't changed. We have.

So why aren't there more prayer meetings in our churches? I'm convinced that the main reason is that pastors know the folks won't come due to their lukewarm spiritual condition. They don't want a lightly attended service that doesn't appear "successful." But can't we start somewhere, even if it means just two or three hearty souls? How can we cast away the idea of a praying church with so many commands and promises staring us in the face?

Where to Begin

Many pastors, I suspect, would like to do better at incorporating prayer into their ministry, but they don't know where or how to begin. I don't know of any magic formula, but I'd like to humbly offer a few suggestions.

First, leaders must lead. Corporate prayer isn't something we can simply delegate to someone else. It has to start with the pastor. Let's purpose in our hearts to get serious about the importance of prayer. Let's spend more time in the Word and study what it says about prayer. And let's ask the Spirit to guide and enlighten us. The very act of wanting to go deeper in prayer will help. We have to start somewhere, even if there's no spiritual fervor or a sense that sometimes God doesn't hear us. The greatest prayer warriors in church history experienced those roadblocks. But by God's grace, they pressed in and pressed on. God honors prayer whether we "feel it" or not.

Second, we can preach a series about answers to prayer in the Bible. How about the time Peter was arrested and thrown in prison? "The church was earnestly praying to God for him. . . . An angel of the Lord appeared. . . . The chains fell off Peter's wrists" (Acts 12:5, 7), and he walked out a free man. That story could be a starting place. The church had little money and no political influence, but God intervened in response to their prayers.

Third, we might also provide time for prayer at the end of Sunday services. Maybe shorten the sermon a bit, and leave time for people to pray with trusted members of leadership.

Finally, we might consider starting a weekly prayer meeting. It may begin small, but God will help it grow. Would he deny us his help if we're trying to build the house of prayer he desires? The Holy Spirit will guide us if we humbly ask. We could invite people to testify to answered prayer in their own lives. This can be done not only at the prayer meeting but also in the Sunday service. When God begins to answer prayers—*which he will*—word will get around, and the fire will spread.

Every spiritual revival that has ever happened has begun with prayer, not special preaching or new methods of "doing church" but simple believers praying for the fire of the Holy Spirit to be kindled among them. Excellent preaching and teaching have often accompanied the revival, but it was earnest prayer that brought down the fire. Our churches are all kindling wood ready to be set aflame as the Holy Spirit visits us in answer to prayer. May God help us to fan the flame of the Holy Spirit's fire in our lives and churches.

CHAPTER 8

Unconditional Surrender

I consider my life worth nothing to me; my only aim is to finish the race and complete the task the Lord Jesus has given me—the task of testifying to the good news of God's grace.

—Acts 20:24

When the Japanese bombed Pearl Harbor on December 7, 1941—the date that Franklin D. Roosevelt said would "live in infamy"—the United States suddenly found itself plunged into a situation it had tried hard to avoid. Things looked grim for the US at that point: the better part of its naval force had been destroyed, and the Germans had honored their treaty with Japan and declared war against the US, effectively forcing the country into two major wars on opposite sides of the globe.

By 1944 the Japanese realized they had picked a fight with the wrong enemy. Their military resources dwindled, as did their force numbers. They grew increasingly desperate. In October of that year, they stunned the world when they unveiled a frightening new weapon. Unable to compete with US air power in either quality or quantity, the Japanese nevertheless started producing flimsy planes as fast as they could. These planes held two deadly secrets. The first was a bomb placed inside the nose of the plane. The second was a pilot who had sworn a sacred oath to the emperor to fly the plane directly into battleships and aircraft carriers. In effect, Japan deployed a massive force of pilot-guided explosive missiles. So many Japanese men were willing to face certain death in dedication to their emperor, whom they held as divine, that the Imperial Japanese Army couldn't build the planes fast enough. The planes—which became known under the name kamikaze ("divine wind")—became a formidable weapon. By the end of the war, kamikazes had flown some 3,800 suicide missions, taking the lives of more than 7,000 Allied sailors and other naval personnel, before Japan finally ran out of the materials necessary to build the planes.

The kamikaze program illustrates an important fact. When you find yourself face-to-face with an opponent who truly doesn't care if they live or die so long as they complete their mission, you have a real problem on your hands. You can't threaten or intimidate them. You can't buy them off or negotiate with them. And when a believer is that dedicated to their mission, they become a powerful weapon in the hand of God.

Paul continued his address to the Ephesian elders, saying, "I consider my life worth nothing to me" (Acts 20:24). Although his friends didn't want to see him chained and thrown into prison, Paul didn't seem to care. He was going to follow Jesus no matter what. I wonder what we would think about Paul if he were around today. Would we accept him? Call him a fanatic? Push him to the sidelines and pretend he's not there?

Or would we be inspired and follow his example?

Eyes on Eternity

We tell ourselves—and we preach to our congregations—that life is just a vapor, while heaven with Christ is eternal. Therefore, we shouldn't consider this life as all-important. But few live that way, right? We live as if this earthly life were forever. As if we couldn't afford to lose it. Yet Scripture declares, "Precious in the sight of the LORD is the death of his faithful servants" (Ps. 116:15).

Our perspective, even as pastors, is often very earthbound. We have our sermons to preach, our programs to administer, our vacations and retirement plans to look forward to. But a far different attitude toward ministry is described in the New Testament. You can see it in the lives of Paul and the other apostles. They had a radical belief in an invisible God and in the eternal rewards that await us when this life is over.

I once visited Hong Kong, where I had been invited to speak to a couple hundred pastors of underground churches in mainland China. I was told that half of them had been in prison because of their allegiance to Christ. I felt unworthy to address them. I thought, "Who am I to talk to them? I've never faced the prospect of being thrown in prison for preaching the gospel of Christ."

The worship was simple but glorious, led by just a couple of guitar players. Something about the way those pastors sang touched me deeply. They looked upward as if they could see Jesus.

I loved the melody of one of the choruses they were singing and asked my interpreter what the words were. I don't have the exact translation, but it went something like this: "Lord, thank you for loving us so much that you came and gave your life for us. And because of your love, we love you back. So we're ready to die. We dedicate our lives to you whether we live or die."

Not exactly the typical praise and worship chorus we hear on a Sunday morning in America.

I found myself praying, "God, is there any way you could get me out of delivering this message? I really would prefer not to speak. I don't feel worthy to teach these people. And their worship is so beautiful. I would rather keep worshiping you with them."

Well, God chose not to excuse me from speaking, and I went ahead with my message. I hope it was helpful to them. But I remember those pastors often when I face a challenge. They were among the happiest Christians I'd ever met. And yet many had to meet in secret. In America we think it's a major trial when the transmission goes bad in our automobile. We live pampered lives compared with those brave soldiers. They had to face the prospect of prison. They were singing, "Yes, Lord, I will gladly die for you." For them that wasn't just a nice sentiment. It was a very real possibility.

Are we familiar with this kind of consecration? "I have only one mission. I want to do the will of God. And if it costs me my life, so be it"? And is that kind of devotion still possible today?

Loving the Forsaken

I want to tell you about a young woman from our church whom I'll call Mary. She was introduced to me several years ago by our missions pastor. "Pastor," he said, "this young woman feels called to the mission field. The other pastors and I have met with her. We think she's ready, and we'd like you to meet her."

I asked him where she wanted to go and what she felt called to do. He said she wasn't sure. She only knew she wanted to go to the Middle East and that she had a burden for people who were forsaken and forgotten.

We prayed for Mary and sent her out. She ended up working mostly among the Yazidi people in the internally displaced people camps in the Middle East. The Yazidis have a primitive animistic religion that the surrounding Muslim population despises. They are treated with contempt by everyone around them, viewed as the offscouring of humanity.[1]

Mary went to teach English, ostensibly, and to work with the Yazidi women. Life is especially brutal for the Yazidi women. When attacked by ISIS forces, they are treated as spoils of war. Yazidi women who convert to Islam are sold as brides. Those who refuse to convert are tortured, raped, and sometimes murdered.

We got regular reports from Mary. The work was going well. Her dedication blessed my heart. She had left everything behind and risked everything to serve Jesus and do his will.

Mary came back to New York for a brief sabbatical about three years later. I asked her how it was going. As she summarized her work among the Yazidis, she casually added a note about a growing difficulty: "Because I'm an outsider, many assume I must be involved in the sex trade. They talk nasty to me. Especially the taxi drivers."

Taxi drivers? Why was she taking taxis? I then learned that was the only way for her to get around. She didn't own a car.

That night, Mary came to our weekly prayer meeting. I brought her up to give an update on her work and then pray for the offering. She shared briefly, describing how she worked with women who were looked down on and treated miserably. She related how she loved them and shared Jesus with them along with teaching English. Then she prayed. Before the collection began, I explained that beyond our regular support, a part of that offering would go to her as a special gift. And I shared her problem and need, telling the group about the taxi drivers who had talked inappropriately to her. "Let's believe God for the car she needs," I said. And then we went on with the service.

Providentially, a group of pastors from Colorado was visiting that night. The instant the meeting ended, they came up to me. "We've just talked together," they said, "and we want to buy Mary the automobile she needs." And they did. Later we sent those pastors a picture of the car they had made possible, and our entire church rejoiced over God's provision for her.

How could we not try to help someone who was serving the Lord, caring little for her own comfort and safety?

Consecrated to God

One word for what Paul discussed in Acts 20:24—considering our lives as worth nothing to ourselves—is *consecration*. To be consecrated means to be dedicated solely and entirely and irrevocably to God. This is what Paul urged the Christians in Rome to do: "Therefore, I urge you, brothers and sisters, in view of God's mercy, to offer your bodies as a living sacrifice, holy and pleasing to God—this is your true and proper worship" (Rom. 12:1).

What God wants most from each one of us is not a financial offering or occasional service in the church. Jesus surrendered himself and died for us, and now he asks us to surrender *our* lives as a pleasing sacrifice to him. What could be more reasonable? After he gave his life for us on the cross, is it enough for us to respond by merely devoting some of our time or a portion of our finances? No. He wants our entire lives to be devoted to him. The kind of consecration we're talking about here must be something we choose to do—a decision we consciously make. God won't compel us to do it against our will. Returning to the warfare theme from the start of this chapter, we have to know that God will not "draft" us into his army. What made the Japanese kamikaze pilots so frightening and dangerous was that they were not forced into fighting; rather, they *voluntarily* swore themselves to obey the emperor.

The nineteenth-century American evangelist Wilbur Chapman said he learned from General William Booth, founder of the Salvation Army, that "the greatness of a man's power is the measure of his surrender."[2] But surrendering our lives is not something we can accomplish on our own. The human spirit never wants to give up its rights in full submission to the Lord. But Jesus regularly commands us to do what is impossible for us. For example, Christ said, "As I have loved you, so you must love one another" (John 13:34). Does he really expect us to love one another with the same exact love he has shown us? Yes! But apart from the power of the Holy Spirit, that kind of love is impossible. Here's the good news: just as *all merit* is in the Son, for he alone gives us acceptance with God, *all power* is by the Spirit, who gives us the willingness and ability to obey all God asks of us. Human effort alone will not suffice.

Just as you and I can't possibly love one another as Christ has loved us without the help of the Holy Spirit, we can't grit our teeth and will ourselves to "offer [our] bodies as a living sacrifice" (Rom. 12:1). As E. M. Bounds said, the power to consecrate can only be communicated by the Holy Ghost. We need to ask God continually for the grace needed to accomplish this consecration: "Lord, give me a heart totally dedicated to you, no matter what."

Blessed Are the Beggars

Think about this for a moment: Before there was any creation, who existed? God. All good that existed was in God. All love that existed was in God. Everything had to come from God, by definition. Then Adam and Eve were created. What was their first consciousness? Has anyone ever been in a better position to appreciate that all things come from God? They could have thought, "We exist because of him. This breath? He gave it to us. All this vegetation, all these animals? He gave them to us." Who else could ever have understood so clearly that everything around them—including their own lives—was a gift?

God's plan of salvation through Christ was to bring us back to that original consciousness—to see and know that everything comes from him and that we were created as receiving vessels only. *He* is the giver of every good and perfect gift (James 1:17). The strongest Christians and the most mature believers are merely the ones who have received the most from God. They have learned the secret that everything must come from the Lord as a gift.

The first thing Jesus taught his followers was, "Blessed are the poor in spirit, for theirs is the kingdom of heaven" (Matt. 5:3). There are two Greek words for "poor" in the New Testament. One indicates someone who has to work hard every day just to buy enough to eat. The other one is used for people who have nothing at all. They can only beg to get through the day. Which word do you think Jesus used in the beatitude? He used the second word. Here's one possible rendering of the beatitude: "Blessed are the *beggars*, for theirs is the kingdom of heaven"! All that God has is available to the beggars because their poverty of spirit makes them dependent on him.

I wish I had known this when I first went into the ministry. It's not about my trying harder to preach better. It's not about better organizing my work and schedule, relying on my own strength. It's all about asking and receiving. Oh, how that reality obliterates our pride! The greatest ministers are the ones who have received the most because they constantly seek God out of their deep sense of need. They can't boast. How can anyone boast in something they had to ask for and receive from God as a gift?

"It's Always Too Soon to Quit"

Paul continued his speech to the Ephesian elders by saying that his only aim was "to finish the race and complete the task the Lord Jesus has given me" (Acts 20:24). It's important to note that he didn't say he wanted to "start" the race or "begin" the task. He didn't say he wanted to "continue" the race or "keep pursuing" the task. He wanted to *finish* the race and *complete* the task.

In almost all ministers' lives, there comes a time when Satan tries to get them to quit before they cross the finish line. When I was only a year or so in the ministry, I was so discouraged I tried to resign from the church. I've already described how bad my preaching was. Plus, we were in a run-down building in a poor neighborhood. The building was nearly empty each week, and the offerings were pitifully low at every service. I felt like I couldn't continue. I didn't succeed in resigning my post, but only because the Lord graciously blocked my way. Twice I tried to do something else to support my family, but in both cases God had the interview appointments canceled at the last moment. I got the message loud and clear: *It's always too soon to quit.*

It's not only in difficult beginnings that we are challenged. Some pastors secretly give up at the other end of the journey. I know people who've been in ministry for twenty-five years or more. They're still in their churches, still drawing their pay, still going through the motions. But deep inside where it counts, they've already retired. One of them said to me, "I don't want to hear about people's problems anymore." Does he still preach? Yes. Is it doctrinally correct? Yes. Is his heart in it? No. He's not really running the race anymore; he's just running out the clock.

In his letter addressed to Philemon, Paul sends regards to "Apphia our sister and Archippus our fellow soldier" (Philem. v. 2). We're not told anything more about either of them. Many commentators believe that Apphia was Philemon's wife and that Archippus was their son. We do know, however, that Archippus had a ministry role in the church at Colossae.

In his letter to the Christians there, Paul wrote, "Tell Archippus: 'See to it that you complete the ministry you have received in the Lord'" (Col. 4:17). These words were read publicly to the church with the rest of the letter. It may have been a gentle rebuke for having neglected some of his duties or a strong word of encouragement to a fellow soldier who had grown weary or discouraged. Either way, Paul tells Archippus to "complete" the ministry the Lord gave him. He had already begun his assignment, but now he needed to *complete* it.

This is a message we can share with those who minister alongside us. It certainly is one we can receive as addressed personally to each of us, who are also Paul's fellow soldiers.

True Success

Paul also says he wants to "complete the task the Lord Jesus has given me" (Acts 20:24). This task is a personal commission Paul received from the Lord. Scripture tells us there is what we might call a "general" will of God: one that applies to all Christians equally. For instance, Jesus told us to "love one another" (John 13:34). That is true for all Christians at all times. Paul said, "It is God's *will* that you should be sanctified; that you should avoid sexual immorality" (1 Thess. 4:3). He also said, "Give thanks in all circumstances; for this is God's *will* for you in Christ Jesus" (1 Thess. 5:18). Every believer should accept these commands as God's will for their life.

But Scripture also makes clear that God has a *personal* will for each of us, involving the unique task that has been given to us and the path we are to follow. Whom should we marry? Where should we live? As believers, where should we serve in the body of Christ? Is the offer to pastor a different church truly from God? Nobody but God knows his individual will for each of us. But thankfully, the Lord *wants* us to know his plan for our lives. As we humbly trust him, he will direct our paths (Prov. 3:5–6).

In light of this, what is the definition of success? Success in life consists of nothing more than finding the will of God and then doing it. If God's will is that you minister in a small town in the upper Midwest, or in a large city, or on a foreign mission field, success for you will mean doing precisely that—regardless of your preferences, or other people's expectations, or the world's definition of having "made it."

Some Christians, though not necessarily called to public ministry, could possibly bring greater joy to God's heart than those in leadership. They have discovered God's plan for their lives and given themselves over to it. That means a deacon or choir member might receive a greater reward than the pastor of the church.

I think we can all agree that Jesus lived his entire life in the perfect will of God. But think about this: What was Jesus doing when he was twenty-seven years old? Was he calling disciples to follow him? Was he healing people? Working miracles? No. He was doing none of those things. But his life was successful because God's perfect will for him was to wait in Nazareth until the right time came to begin his public ministry. It is noteworthy that when John was baptizing Jesus in the Jordan River, *before* he entered public ministry, Jesus heard the Father say, "This is my Son, whom I love; with him I am well pleased" (Matt. 3:17).

Too many ministers have the idea that success is nothing more than the carnal "American dream"—advancement, fame, fortune—and their model for success is someone wearing $400 sneakers, living extravagantly, and hanging out with celebrities and politicians. What they call "great" is actually a sign that they've lost their way.

God's will for your life is between you and him. Each day you can simply walk with the one who sent you on your mission. Draw near to him. Listen to the Spirit's voice. Desiring approval from people can be a trap. In the end, the approval you need must come from Jesus.

Are you in the perfect will of God today? Are you seeking to know this personal plan for your life, a plan that existed even before you were born? Do you trust the Holy Spirit for the grace to do the will of God as it is revealed to you? The highest form of worshiping God has nothing to do with singing praise choruses or lying prostrate on the floor. What the Lord delights in most is that which was written concerning his own Son:

> When Christ came into the world, he said:
>
> > "Sacrifice and offering you did not desire,
> > > but a body you prepared for me;
> > with burnt offerings and sin offerings
> > > you were not pleased.
> > Then I said, 'Here I am—it is written about me in
> > > the scroll—
> > > *I have come to do your will, my God.*'" (Heb.
> > > 10:5–7)

Sometimes doing the will of God is not so easy. I remember an instance many years ago when I found myself at ten o'clock on a Saturday night with no sermon for Sunday. No matter what I tried, the heavens seemed as brass—not a word. I prayed, "God, please help me. Is something in me hindering your Spirit?" Immediately, God brought to mind my relationship with three people who had grown distant to me. It's as if a silent wall had been erected. No big fight or feud, just a sense that something wasn't the way it should be.

I sensed that God was saying, "Call them and ask for forgiveness."

"What? Call them? Now? Isn't it too late in the evening for that? And you know, in two cases for sure, they're the ones needing to apologize." My pride was ruffled at the idea that I was somehow in the wrong.

"Do you want my blessing? Then do my will. Make it right."

I took a deep breath and called the first person. I secretly hoped he wouldn't pick up. But he did.

"Uh, hi," I said. "It's Jim."

"Hi, how are you?"

"I'm good. Listen, there's something I want to say to you. I have this gnawing feeling that something may be wrong between us. If there's anything I've said or done that hurt you or offended you, I'm sorry. Please forgive me."

To my surprise, he said, "Frankly, I've had the same feeling. There's nothing you've done that you need to apologize for. But if there's anything I've done that has hurt *you*, I apologize as well." We had a brief prayer together, and that was that. The same thing happened with the other two people.

I felt that a great burden had been lifted. And, yes, I did get direction and help for the next day. Was it hard to make those calls? Absolutely. But God has promised us grace to accomplish his will.

I have been blessed to have traveled a lot in my life, not only around our country but also on numerous trips overseas. There are some beautiful places on this earth, but let me tell you about the best place you could ever live in—the center of God's will. Will there be satanic attacks? For sure. Challenging days filled with mountains blocking your way? Absolutely. But the joy is inexpressible, and the peace you find there is fathomless. We will never be happier than when we're in the center of God's will. That, brothers and sisters in Christ, is the true measure of success.

CHAPTER 9

KEEP WATCH

Keep watch over yourselves and all the flock of which the Holy Spirit has made you overseers. Be shepherds of the church of God, which he bought with his own blood. I know that after I leave, savage wolves will come in among you and will not spare the flock. Even from your own number men will arise and distort the truth in order to draw away disciples after them. So be on your guard!

—ACTS 20:28-31

Anyone who has ever flown on a commercial airliner has heard "the talk." Shortly before takeoff, the flight attendants get up and tell the passengers about the airplane's safety features. They point out the location of the exit doors. They show how to buckle and unbuckle the seat belt. They explain how to put on the inflatable life vest. They demonstrate the emergency oxygen mask, show how it drops from the overhead compartment, and describe how to place it over the nose and mouth and continue to breathe normally. Finally, they instruct each passenger to be sure to put on their own mask before helping children or others with their masks. The reason for this last injunction is that if we fail to protect our own lives, those who depend on us may lose theirs as well.

Paul made a similar point when he first cautioned the elders in Ephesus to keep watch over themselves before he instructed them to keep watch over the flock. Paul knew that Satan is cunning. Our enemy knows that if he can take down the shepherd, the sheep are easily scattered and more vulnerable to his attacks. All Christians are engaged in spiritual warfare, but the devil attacks ministers with special vigor.

It's all the more diabolical because it's harder for pastors to share about their spiritual battles. They fear—not without reason—that people will be scandalized by the idea that their pastor could struggle spiritually. "What? You were tempted to lie? I thought you were a minister!" I had that belief when I was growing up. Pastors never had fights with their wives, I thought; they were never tempted with lust. Some people in ministry play into this belief, setting themselves up as a breed apart. But we all know too well how misguided this kind of thinking is.

John Wesley, the founder of Methodism, was one of the great Christian leaders of the eighteenth century. His lifetime achievements for the cause of Christ are almost beyond belief. Unfortunately, against counsel from those close to him, he married a woman who badgered him constantly and even took his private papers and revealed them to his critics and enemies. He ended up writing to her, "Dear wife, I dislike not being safe in my own house . . . I cannot call even my study, even my bureau, my own."[1] This was a man under great strain. Think of the discouragements he must have faced, as well as the temptation to distrust God or go into an angry rage.

What goes into this "keeping watch over ourselves" that Paul finds so important as he cautions the church leaders he loves so much? First, through the grace of God, we need to humbly take stock of our own spiritual walk with Christ. We should ask ourselves, "How do I spend my time away from church? What kind of intimacy do I have with the Lord? How much time do I spend in the Word? Do I read it merely to get sermon material? Or do I meditate on it for my own spiritual nourishment?"

Our co-laborers in the work of the Lord can also help us to remain vigilant over our lives and ministries. Besides having open communication with the pastoral staff, I have found it beneficial to cultivate relationships with ministers outside our church whom I respect and trust. People with whom I can be candid about challenges I'm facing. People who won't shy away from telling me when they sense that something is amiss. Over the years, I've made it a practice to bring those trusted others to preach at our church. I ask them to tell me honestly what they discern that might not be pleasing to God. I know they won't tell me what I *want* to hear. They'll speak the truth in love as to what I *need* to hear.

Shepherd the Shepherds

The reason we keep watch over ourselves is so that we can better keep watch over "all the flock of which the Holy Spirit has made [us] overseers" and to be "shepherds of the church of God, which he bought with his own blood" (Acts 20:28).

That includes shepherding the church staff. We need to keep watch over those who labor alongside us and under our authority. We need to spend time with them and encourage them. I learned this the hard way.

Many years ago, in one of our staff meetings, I asked one of the other pastors to lead us in prayer. He couldn't do it. He couldn't get the words out. He even broke down and started crying. I should have discerned that something was seriously wrong. When someone is unable to pray publicly, it's most likely because something is wrong spiritually. But I missed it. I didn't follow up on the warning signals that were there.

A month later Carol and I were away on vacation. A close friend was preaching at our church while we were away. He called me late after the service and said, "You'd better get back here."

"Why?" I said. "We just got here three days ago."

"Well," my friend said, "your associate pastor just emptied the church bank account and ran off with a woman in the church. Her two children are with her husband. It looks like she's abandoned them." I learned too late that the poor man was deluded, and so was the woman. He had left a note for me that said God was "leading" them into a new season of their lives! Pain and bewilderment followed for the families involved.

I'd give anything to have that staff meeting over again. Maybe if I'd been more spiritually alert, I could have headed off this disaster. Or maybe not—the situation was pretty far gone by that point. But I learned a painful lesson about the importance of staying alert to the spiritual condition of those on staff.

There was once a young man in our church who had been saved out of a life of drug addiction. Eventually he became an usher. He was a hard worker, very dedicated. He assisted in the collection of the offering, helping with the count, making sure everything ran smoothly. I later learned that for all his active participation, he rarely came to church on a Sunday just to sit in the service. Keeping himself "too busy" to participate in the services did not help him to resist the temptation to go back into drug use. And once he did go back to his old ways, he made sure to stay busy to hide what was wrong. Some people, when they backslide, prefer to stay occupied during a service, doing anything other than having to sit through the meeting. That way they can avoid hearing the Word and the conviction they know will come with it.

We now have a policy for everyone who serves in the Sunday services: if someone serves, they have to sit and worship with the congregation in at least one service. We deeply appreciate all who serve, but they can't always be giving; they have to be spiritually receiving also.

Feed, Guide, Protect

Keeping watch over the flock is challenging, whether that flock numbers in the dozens, hundreds, or thousands. Shepherds do three things: they feed the flock, they guide the flock, and they protect the flock.

We discussed feeding the flock in a previous chapter, which mainly had to do with teaching and preaching to them the whole counsel of God. But it's not enough to have our congregants hear a Bible-based sermon once a week. They have to receive daily nourishment from God's Word. They have to "crave pure spiritual milk, so that by it [they] may grow up in [their] salvation" (1 Peter 2:2). We can't just eat one big meal on Sunday and then go without food for the rest of the week. In the same way, the best sermon in the world can't sustain a believer until the following Sunday. We have to teach our people the vital importance of being strengthened daily by biblical truth. This is a critical point, given that in America, "between early 2019 and 2020, the percentage of US adults who say they use the Bible daily dropped from 14 percent to 9 percent, according to the State of the Bible 2020 report released . . . by the Barna Group and the American Bible Society."[2]

Spiritual Accountability

The idea of shepherding also brings up the question of spiritual accountability. Is there a foolproof accountability system to keep believers, including ourselves, on the straight and narrow?

Let's review Christian living as outlined in the New Testament. The first and most important task is to spread the gospel and bring people into the kingdom. When that happens, the Holy Spirit comes to live inside the new believers. Ultimately, only the power of the indwelling Spirit can produce victorious Christian living. That is why Paul declared, "So I say, walk by the Spirit, and you will not gratify the desires of the flesh" (Gal. 5:16). The flesh, or sinful nature, means Jim Cymbala apart from God's Spirit. If we can encourage and help people to walk with the Lord and yield to the Spirit daily and hourly, what will be the result? The "love, joy, peace, forbearance, kindness, goodness, faithfulness, gentleness and self-control" (Gal. 5:22–23) that the Spirit produces. Yielding to the Spirit is the only antidote to the selfish, sinful nature. In fact, God never works with the "old Jim Cymbala." Improvement and reformation are impossible for that self-centered person. Only living by the indwelling Spirit will give us victory. Teaching alone, no matter how biblical, can never be a substitute.

So what's the benefit of "accountability systems"? They're helpful but never foolproof. We've probably all dealt with sincere people who get ensnared by sin that holds them captive. Isn't it true that if a person really wants to go backward and indulge the flesh, no human control system will stop them? If they're part of an accountability group, they'll either hide their behavior or lie about it. It's that obvious and simple. Remember Paul's catalog of the works of the flesh: "sexual immorality, impurity and debauchery; idolatry and witchcraft; hatred, discord, jealousy, fits of rage, selfish ambition, dissensions, factions and envy; drunkenness, orgies, and the like" (Gal. 5:19–21). Let's be real. If a believer gets involved in these kinds of things, why would they hesitate to lie about it? No, only the power of the Holy Spirit working daily in a humble, believing heart can keep a person from going backward.

The same goes for the idea that personal discipleship by a mature·believer will automatically produce a steadfast faith in others. Let's consider the example of Jesus Christ himself. He called twelve men to be his disciples. They lived with him and traveled with him for more than three years. He was the ultimate teacher and discipler. What lessons he must have taught them, and what an example he set. But even all that couldn't stop them from forsaking him on the night he was arrested. Judas betrayed him, Peter denied him, and all of them ran away when he was arrested and nailed to the cross.

Paul had assistants in the ministry—some of whom he had probably led to the Lord. Some traveled with him and sat under his powerful ministry. Timothy was a prime example. He was placed as a leader in the church at Ephesus, but Paul must have heard of Timothy's problem with fear. He had to admonish him with 2 Timothy 1:6–7: "For this reason I remind you to fan into flame the gift of God, which is in you through the laying on of my hands. For the Spirit God gave us does not make us timid, but gives us power, love and self-discipline." Paul's past teaching and his personal letter couldn't solve Timothy's problem. It was only the fire of the Spirit that would give power, love, and self-discipline.

On the other hand, Demas, another worker, was with Paul when Paul was imprisoned in Rome for two years (Col. 4:14; Philem. 1:24). But Paul later sadly reported that "Demas, because he loved this world, has deserted me and has gone to Thessalonica" (2 Tim. 4:10). How could someone sit under the apostle Paul and travel with him yet desert the cause of Christ? This is doubly alarming, since John declares, "Do not love the world or anything in the world. If anyone loves the world, love for the Father is not in them" (1 John 2:15). What could have happened to Demas?

These examples remind us that Christianity is not primarily a teaching religion like the Mormons and Jehovah's Witnesses. All they can do is drill erroneous doctrine into the heads of their followers. True Christianity is about the supernatural power of God, delivering us and keeping us on a daily basis. Teaching, preaching, and discipleship have their place, but they can never replace God himself.

Encouragement and Support

Instead of relying solely on accountability systems, although they might be helpful, God directs us to "encourage one another daily, as long as it is called 'Today,' so that none of you may be hardened by sin's deceitfulness" (Heb. 3:13). It's all about Jesus being at the center of our lives. As we trust him, he will never fail. *"To him who is able to keep you from stumbling* and to present you before his glorious presence without fault and with great joy—to the only God our Savior be glory, majesty, power and authority, through Jesus Christ our Lord, before all ages, now and forevermore!" (Jude vv. 24–25).

Some years ago Carol had a member in the choir—I'll call him André—who had come to the Lord from a life of sexual immorality, and he still dealt with powerful temptation from time to time. André would sometimes come over to Carol during a choir practice break, and he would say to her, "Please pray for me; I'm struggling." He was open about his struggles, and my wife would pray and encourage him. But at the end of the night, he would leave the church with everyone else and have to face the hard streets of New York City, with all their temptations and challenges. Yet week after week, month after month, and, yes, year after year, God not only kept André but also turned him into a mature man of God. He ended up with a beautiful wife and family that served the Lord. In the end, it was neither Carol nor I as his pastor who kept André accountable; it was the grace of God as André clung to him in faith.

Hardship Is Coming

Paul said, "I know that after I leave, savage wolves will come in among you and will not spare the flock. Even from your own number men will arise and distort the truth in order to draw away disciples after them" (Acts 20:29–30). There are several lessons to learn from this.

First, notice the words *I know*. Paul *knew*, through revelation by the Holy Spirit, what the future held for the elders in Ephesus. And yet he didn't presume to be able to stop events from happening or to "rebuke" them away. Like it or not, these difficult moments were coming. When God speaks about the future, it is never "negative," but rather the guaranteed reality of future events that he is preparing us to face.

In Matthew 24, Jesus describes what will happen in the last days: Wars. Famines. Earthquakes. In particular, he said of his followers, "You will be handed over to be persecuted and put to death, and you will be hated by all nations because of me. At that time many will turn away from the faith and will betray and hate each other, and many false prophets will appear and deceive many people" (Matt. 24:9–11). Again, there is no hint that Christians can simply refuse to receive these things or can bind them in the power of Jesus's name. These are not just possibilities for the future of planet earth and his people, but rather events guaranteed to happen. Some situations in our lives can be turned around by the prayer of faith. But we need to accept that other events foretold by God himself are inevitable. We can only prepare both ourselves and our people for them. As Paul said, "So be on your guard!" (Acts 20:31).

The second lesson is that we should not be knocked off balance by news that hardship is coming. And we should teach the flock the same.

> Do not fret because of those who are evil
>> or be envious of those who do wrong;
> for like the grass they will soon wither,
>> like green plants they will soon die away. . . .
>
> Be still before the LORD
>> and wait patiently for him;
> do not fret when people succeed in their ways,
>> when they carry out their wicked schemes.
>
> Refrain from anger and turn from wrath;
>> do not fret—it leads only to evil.
> For those who are evil will be destroyed,
>> but those who hope in the LORD will inherit
>> the land. (Ps. 37:1–2, 7–9)

Will evil continue to spread across the earth? Will people continue to succeed in their wicked schemes? Of course. But does that mean we can't effectively evangelize? That there can't be spiritual revival in our churches? Won't God do wonderful things among us if we humble ourselves and pray? Of course he will.

Our goal is not to defeat secular humanism or attempt to

make America a holy nation. There is only one holy nation, and that is the church of Jesus Christ. Let's aim for winning souls one at a time. And let's remember the words Mary spoke to the servants at the wedding in Cana: "Do whatever he tells you" (John 2:5). Now *we* are his servants; and if we obey his directions, we will see his supernatural power at work again.

Let's also remember that we're going home soon. Then it will all be over. No more sin, Satan, pain, or death. Only eternity with Christ and fellowship with all the believers who have preceded us. Let's comfort our flocks with these words amid the hardships they may be facing.

Savage Wolves

In his address to the Ephesian elders, Paul said "savage wolves" would come in and not spare the flock. These two-legged wolves are more dangerous than anything found in the wild, since they will try to bring false doctrines into the church. The startling fact is that some will come "from your own number" (Acts 20:30)! The danger Paul is describing comes from those who claim to be Christian teachers. They don't deny the Word of God outright, but rather "distort the truth," with the goal of winning a personal following. This danger was so real that for three years Paul "never stopped warning each of you night and day with tears" (Acts 20:31). Clearly, this was a real and present danger to the flock.

I sometimes find myself watching cable TV stations that feature religious programming. Some of what I find there is good and it blesses me. Sound biblical preaching is always inspiring. But much of what I view is heretical. I often think, "How many unbelievers are watching and thinking that this represents the Christian faith?" And how do we know that some of our precious believers aren't being taken in by one of these charlatans? Or sending money to one of the con artists with their "seed faith" formula aimed only at lining their own pocket? Do we, as pastors, have a duty to warn them about such things?

I know that many of us are reluctant to take that approach. We'd rather focus on teaching the Word and maintaining a positive tone. Also, we don't want to be accused of being "judgmental." That's a wise approach in most matters. But we have to be careful not to fall into what a friend of mine called the love trap of "sloppy agape." This happens when, in the name of love and harmony, we fail to speak out and warn people about genuinely dangerous teachings.

Jesus said, "Watch out for false prophets. They come to you in sheep's clothing, but inwardly they are ferocious wolves. By their fruit you will recognize them" (Matt. 7:15–16). Notice the strong language from God's Son. He called them "ferocious wolves." Many today would recoil at such language. "Judgmental!" "Where's your love?" "Hate speech!" But this warning came from the mouth of our Savior, Jesus Christ, who saw ahead to what was coming down the pike to harm his church.

Notice the warning from Paul against false teachers *distorting* the truth. He doesn't refer to *denying* the truth—that would be easier to identify. Spotting distortion is always more difficult. They don't deny Jesus; they just talk about a different Jesus. They don't deny the Bible; they will even quote from it. But Satan did the same thing when he tempted Jesus in the desert. These wolves pervert Scripture; they twist it to mean something other than the truth of the gospel.

The Flock God Cherishes

So what is the reason behind Paul's admonition to watch ourselves and the congregations we shepherd? Why are the wolves called "savage"? They are dangerous because their target is the flock God cherishes. The sheep under our spiritual care were all "bought with his own blood" (Acts 20:28), and they make up the "church of God" (Gal. 1:13), which was made possible through the agonies of Christ on the cross. They are all intensely loved by God, who knows every intricacy of their lives—every fear, every problem, every weakness. If only one person were on earth, God still would have sent his Son to die for that one solitary soul. Every sermon and service, every conversation and counseling session, involves at least one of the sheep God entrusted to us. Anyone who loves one of my children or grandchildren and shows unusual kindness to them immediately finds a special place in my heart. If our parental love results in such appreciation, how must God feel when we labor to feed and guide and protect his beloved flock? Let us give ourselves to being the shepherds God wants us to be.

CHAPTER 10

DIVISION IS DEADLY

*I appeal to you, brothers and sisters, in the
name of our Lord Jesus Christ, that all of you
agree with one another in what you say and
that there be no divisions among you.*

—1 CORINTHIANS 1:10

In 1828, when he was nineteen, and again in 1831, Abraham Lincoln paddled flatboats down the Mississippi River to New Orleans. By many accounts, his lifelong hatred of the institution of slavery was born through his firsthand exposure to the slave market in New Orleans during these visits. The issue of slavery burned in the United States for the rest of Lincoln's life. Southerners, by and large, were adamantly in favor of it; most Northerners were vehemently opposed.

In 1858 Lincoln delivered his famous "house divided" speech, which gained him national exposure and later a nomination as the presidential candidate for the newly formed, antislavery Republican party, eventually taking him to the White House. Lincoln made it clear where he stood. The nation, he said, couldn't endure "half slave and half free"; inevitably it would "become all one thing or the other." And he said, "A house divided against itself cannot stand."[1]

Lincoln was quoting Jesus Christ (Mark 3:25), even though Lincoln was one of only two US presidents with no religious affiliation. The original context was that Jesus had healed people and cast out demons on the Sabbath. The Jewish authorities were incensed at his actions, saying, "He is possessed by Beelzebul! By the prince of demons he is driving out demons" (Mark 3:22).

Jesus could have simply denied this accusation. But he knew his denial would fall on deaf ears. He could also have taken the occasion to explain who he actually was: the Son of God. But in God's plan, it wasn't yet time for that declaration. Instead, Jesus responded by pointing out the logical fallacy of his opponents: "Jesus called them over to him and began to speak to them in parables: 'How can Satan drive out Satan? If a kingdom is divided against itself, that kingdom cannot stand. If a house is divided against itself, that house cannot stand. And if Satan opposes himself and is divided, he cannot stand; his end has come'" (Mark 3:23–26).

How could Jesus be on Satan's side and yet cast out evil spirits? Satan would never tolerate such disunity.

Division Brings Weakness

The principle is simple: division brings weakness. We have all seen it time and time again, in every imaginable context. Disunity undermines families, military units, sports teams, you name it. Any grouping that is divided against itself ultimately cannot stand.

This principle certainly applies to churches. A church pursuing genuine New Testament goals—spiritual growth, evangelism, being a house of prayer, honoring God's Word, and so on—can't be effective if it is divided against itself. Even an undercurrent of division and strife will weaken that body of believers. The pastor of such a church ends up on a treadmill, expending a lot of effort and energy but making little progress. We can fast and pray, we can study our Bibles, we can do anything we like. But if there's ongoing division in a church, that church is in a precarious position. It may be able to grow in numbers for a season; it may be capable of staging entertaining services. But ultimately a church divided against itself, a staff divided against itself, can never enjoy the full blessing of God and will eventually crumble if gone unchecked. This is why Paul admonished the New Testament churches to seek unity: "I appeal to you, brothers and sisters, in the name of our Lord Jesus Christ, that all of you agree with one another in what you say and that there be *no divisions among you*, but that you be perfectly *united* in mind and thought" (1 Cor. 1:10).

We too rarely see that kind of dedication to unity in our churches. When we know there is division among us, we often look the other way and pretend it isn't there. Or worse, we let our unity in Christ be subordinated to other causes or identities in the culture.

Pandemic Pandemonium

This kind of division became painfully apparent during the COVID-19 pandemic. You might have hoped that a crisis of this nature and magnitude would have called forth a wave of unity among believers, that we would place our concern for our Christian brothers and sisters ahead of other considerations. And in some places, that happened. But in others, the pandemic revealed more clearly than ever that too many people who claim to be believers don't identify themselves first as Christians. They identify themselves primarily as Black or Hispanic or White or Asian. They identify first as Democrats or Republicans, conservatives or progressives.

I know firsthand of churches that suffered division and fractured relationships because they supported one political group or movement over another. I know of churches that lost members because they required people to wear face masks to church or because they allowed people to come to church without masks. There are churches across America right now whose congregants are fighting over the value of vaccinations. Behind it all, Satan is subtly orchestrating this division in the church of Christ.

Instead of agreeing to disagree on political and cultural matters, many so-called believers have used social media to engage in the character assassination of their own brothers and sisters in Christ. They have even aligned themselves with hostile, anti-Christian groups that deny the Word of God. How can we reconcile this ugly vitriol with Scripture? "This is how we know who the children of God are and who the children of the devil are: Anyone who does not do what is right is not God's child, nor is anyone who does not love their brother and sister. . . . We know that we have passed from death to life, because we love each other. . . . Anyone who hates a brother or sister is a murderer, and you know that no murderer has eternal life residing in him" (1 John 3:10, 14–15).

Think of that! If we're not loving, forgiving, and supporting another believer, God calls it hatred. There is no in-between state of lukewarm toleration or purposeful separation that we can redefine as "love." And it's not doctrinal correctness or the gifts of the Spirit that prove we're true Christians. Not at all. "By this everyone will know that you are my disciples, if you love one another" (John 13:35).

It is now clearer than ever that too many churches are built more on racial, ethnic, or political factors than identification with Jesus. Believers fuss and fight with each other just as non-Christians do. Does anyone really believe that unbelievers have the solution to the hatred and prejudice so rampant in our culture and world? Political parties and conservative or liberal philosophies can't change one human heart, and that's where hatred and anger live in all of us. We should pass every legislation we can to bring equal opportunity and protection to all our citizens. But I'm afraid that national problems aren't the deep disease that Christ is most concerned about.

The Dark Stain of Racism

To our shame, more than 150 years after the Civil War, racism is still a powerful force in America, and one that infects many sectors of Christ's church. Across America, for the most part, Black churches stay Black, and White churches stay White.

When city neighborhoods change, White churches are quick to move to the suburbs. If those suburbs change, they move even farther away. Often this has been done with the lame excuse that to have church growth you must have a "homogeneous" congregation. Intelligent people know that is a code word for racism. It's just another way of saying we want to have some distance from those who are "other."

The problem goes both ways.

Our church has always welcomed people from all races and ethnicities and economic backgrounds. Sadly, some of our Black members have told us that relatives and friends from other churches criticize them, saying, "I can't believe you'd go to a church where the Man is the pastor." That mentality is not an example of Christian love and unity.

Scripture says heaven is populated by "a great multitude

that no one could count, from every nation, tribe, people and language, standing before the throne and before the Lamb" (Rev. 7:9). Why would God send anyone to that kind of heaven for eternity to mix with the very people they purposely avoided on earth? How can we discriminate against any person Christ died for, whether White, Black, Asian, or any other race or ethnicity? How can unrepentant "haters" spend eternity with God, who is perfect love?

And here is an important question for pastors. How can we get up each Sunday and declare the gospel that begins with "God so loved the world," if we're not sincerely anxious for every person—no matter their race or ethnicity—to enter our buildings and be genuinely loved? What an indictment of the ministry when preachers of all races appeal to the lowest instincts of anger and prejudice among their people!

Here's the reality we too often choose to ignore: When God looks down from heaven, he doesn't see races and ethnicities and "demographics." He sees people. People his Son died for. People he wants to save and bring into his family. Here's the bottom line, pastors: If you don't want to welcome into your church everyone Christ died for, take down the cross from your building. Please. If you're not willing to welcome and minister to everyone Jesus died to save—homeless, wealthy, poor, Black, White, Latino, gay, straight—how can you possibly claim to be a Christian church? How can you reconcile that attitude with the love of God?

One Lord, One Faith, One Baptism

Tragically, the church has a long history not only of tolerating division but of encouraging it, even building it into our very structures. Any smart unbeliever can see the enormous disconnect between what we claim to be and what we actually are.

We defend the authority of Scripture, yet the Word of God itself declares, "There is one body and one Spirit, just as you were called to one hope when you were called; one Lord, one faith, one baptism; one God and Father of all, who is over all and through all and in all" (Eph. 4:4–6).

One faith? One body? Doctrinal and denominational differences have splintered the church of Christ for centuries. After the Protestant Reformation, religious wars were fought not only between Protestant and Roman Catholic forces but also between Lutheran and Reformed armies—all claiming allegiance to Christ. Imagine people being persecuted and killed in the name of more orthodox Christian doctrine! It must have made the angels weep.

Sadly, many of us are more sectarian than we are Christian. We're more Arminian or Pentecostal or Calvinist than we are New Testament Christian. Yes, there will always be differences in doctrinal emphasis and style. But can't these all exist within an overall context of love and unity? That ideal is worlds apart from the enmity, strife, accusation, backbiting, and criticism we often see among believers. Why not be supportive of other faithful Christians even if they don't do everything the same way we do? Instead, we let ourselves become estranged over secondary matters. Not over the divinity of Jesus or salvation through faith in Christ alone, but over differences that could easily be accommodated among people who genuinely love God and one another.

My study of church history has shown me that no matter their denominational distinctives, men and women who are dedicated to Christ and filled with the Word and the Holy Spirit have always made an impression on their world. This can be proved by the untold number of people over the centuries who brought honor to Christ while differing on secondary matters. Take, for example, the friendship between Wesley and Whitefield. Wesley abhorred the

Calvinism Whitefield believed in, and Whitefield didn't subscribe to Wesley's Arminianism. But they loved each other. More importantly, God used them both. So does God support Calvinism or Arminianism? Maybe neither . . . or maybe both.

Is Christ Divided?

I once received a letter from a man who had visited our church. He said, "I've read your books and enjoyed my visit to your church on Sunday, but I now have lost all confidence in you. You actually had a woman in the choir come up and pray for the offering!" I still haven't found where the Bible clearly states that having a woman pray in church is contrary to God's heart. God said, "Your sons and daughters will prophesy" (Acts 2:17), but a woman can't pray for the offering? Nevertheless, if that's what a church thinks is important, then so be it. But to lambaste another Christian church over that point? To take another example, I have never found a passage that mandates how often communion must be served. Some churches do it weekly, some monthly, some less frequently. I'm sure they all have reasons for why they follow their particular approach. But in the absence of any clear scriptural direction, how can we treat those who differ on secondary matters as heretics? With unbelievers around us dying daily without Christ, is squabbling the best way to spend our time?

Someone once said, "If Christians agree on ninety-five percent of what they believe, then why do they argue so much about the other five percent?" Why indeed? Why do we major in minors? Remember what Paul wrote to the church in Corinth:

> My brothers and sisters, some from Chloe's household have informed me that there are quarrels among you. What I mean is

this: One of you says, "I follow Paul"; another, "I follow Apollos"; another, "I follow Cephas"; still another, "I follow Christ."

Is Christ divided? Was Paul crucified for you? Were you baptized in the name of Paul? (1 Cor. 1:11–13)

Paul said he couldn't address the Corinthians as people who lived by the Spirit, but as people who were still worldly (1 Cor. 3:1). Why?

Since there is jealousy and quarreling among you, are you not worldly? Are you not acting like mere humans? For when one says, "I follow Paul," and another, "I follow Apollos," are you not mere human beings?

What, after all, is Apollos? And what is Paul? Only servants, through whom you came to believe—as the Lord has assigned to each his task. I planted the seed, Apollos watered it, but God has been making it grow. So neither the one who plants nor the one who waters is anything, but only God, who makes things grow. (1 Cor. 3:3–7)

To Paul, an emphasis on belonging to him or to Apollos was a sign of carnality, not of maturity or doctrinal purity. Isn't an undue emphasis on being evangelical or Reformed or charismatic the same thing?

What are you and I to do about all this division? Few of us are in a position to make major structural changes. But we can do our part by being open and accepting of all born-again Christians regardless of what church they go to. We can also start rooting for one another. The best way to grieve the Holy Spirit is when we proclaim, "We're the only ones," or, "We're not the only ones, but we really are special!"

Division in the Local Church

Now let's talk about conflict that might hit a little closer to home. Division also kills within our local churches—just as it does in the larger context of the body of Christ.

For years, pastors in the United States were healthier than those in other professions. They contracted fewer diseases, had fewer accidents, and lived longer than most other people. There was even a joke that pastors were the last people to get into heaven because they lived so long. But clergy health started going downhill in the 1960s. Pastors started gaining weight, experiencing stress, and suffering from diseases such as diabetes, arthritis, asthma, heart disease, and other chronic conditions at an alarming rate.[2] There are many reasons for this shift. But I'm convinced that the major factor is the stress that comes from dealing with disputes and disunity within their own churches.

Division can crop up anywhere: in the church board, in the worship team, in the pastoral staff, and of course among individuals and families. Part of the reason why dealing with division can take such a toll on the pastor is that it involves confronting people who are divisive, and most pastors want to avoid that! They don't want to risk having people from one side of the dispute—or even from both sides—leave the church and take other people (and their tithes) with them. So they walk on eggshells, tiptoe around land mines, trim their sermons—all to make sure they don't trigger any outbursts. They put up with all manner of gossip, slander, and discord to avoid confrontation. Of course, other members of the church are aware of the divisiveness around them and wonder why the pastor isn't addressing it. In reality, most leaders try to avoid rocking the boat so they can meet budgets and make the payroll.

But here's our dilemma: problems don't go away by themselves. Divisiveness doesn't heal itself. If you don't deal with it today, you'll inevitably have to deal with it later. And by then it will be worse.

Dealing with Division

We can't completely prevent divisive behavior in the church, any more than we can eradicate other forms of carnality. But there are some things we can do.

We can start by reminding ourselves that the only cure for division is something we've discussed previously. The fruit of the Holy Spirit is the antidote that overcomes the proud, selfish tendencies in all of us. It is striking that Paul's list of the works of the flesh includes numerous sins that are at the heart of disunity: "hatred, discord, jealousy, fits of rage, selfish ambition, dissensions, factions and envy" (Gal. 5:20–21). Conversely, what makes up the fruit of the Spirit includes the basic ingredients of unity: "love, joy, peace, forbearance, [and] kindness" (Gal. 5:22). Paul also taught that true unity must be nurtured and protected: "I urge you to live a life worthy of the calling you have received. Be completely humble and gentle; be patient, bearing with one another in love. *Make every effort* to keep the unity of the Spirit through the bond of peace" (Eph. 4:1–3).

Second, we shouldn't preach only *against* division but also *for* unity. But note that it is best to do this *before* division arises. If we wait until an eruption has occurred, folks can feel we're trying to patch a bandage over the problem. It's better to try to preach and pray for the unity of the Spirit before trouble starts.

Third, we must be vigilant against slander and gossip. In my experience, these are the biggest culprits in creating division and strife. Every few months, on a Sunday, we present to the church the people who have recently been accepted as new members. In my remarks before the whole congregation, I always remind the new members, "If you hear anyone speak an unkind word about an usher, a choir member, a member of our staff, or another member of the church without that person present, you have authority from me to stop them midsentence and say, 'Hold on. That's not God's solution to the problem. If someone has hurt you, go to them directly and try to resolve it. If that fails, let's bring the matter to the pastor, and he'll bring you together with the person who may have hurt you so that you can pray and get things right.'"

Does this eliminate all slander and gossip? No. But it hopefully reduces it and makes it easier to address future situations. Most importantly, it's the right thing to do before God for the sake of his church.

Fourth, you can pray that God will grant the unity of the Spirit within your staff. Sadly, many pastors have to deal with divisive behavior among those closest to them. Often the cause is old-fashioned jealousy. "Anger is cruel and fury overwhelming, but who can stand before jealousy?" (Prov. 27:4). You know what it sounds like: "Why don't I get more chances to teach?" "Why is *he* leading worship?" "Why wasn't *my* work acknowledged publicly?"

A common mistake we make is seeking to hire people who are smart and talented, with little concern about their humility and kindness. Looking for the most gifted people available is wise. But first we must search for people who are spiritually mature and teachable. These are not qualities that appear on a résumé or a transcript. It takes prayer and discernment to identify them.

Notice the confrontational attitude that Paul outlines in dealing with divisive people: "I urge you, brothers and sisters, to watch out for those who cause divisions and put obstacles in your way that are contrary to the teaching you have learned. Keep away from them. For such people are not serving our Lord Christ, but their own appetites. By smooth talk and flattery they deceive the minds of naive people" (Rom. 16:17–18).

And he instructed Titus, "Warn a divisive person once, and then warn them a second time. After that, have nothing to do with them. You may be sure that such people are warped and sinful; they are self-condemned" (Titus 3:10–11).

Perhaps while you've been reading this chapter, the Holy Spirit has reminded you of hurtful division in your staff, churches, or even in family relationships. I have no easy formula to follow, but I know God will help you in bringing healing and unity to your situation. Stop for a moment and admit that the problem is there. Only God can help. Ask for the grace needed to confront the offending parties in love. This requires wisdom from heaven, for it involves delicate spiritual surgery. God will honor your efforts to restore the unity of the Spirit in the bond of peace.

Division in the church does more damage to the cause of Christ than secularism and witchcraft combined. When the church is united in faith and prayer, no worldly or demonic forces can stop us from expanding Christ's kingdom.

CHAPTER 11

MONEY

I have not coveted anyone's silver or gold or clothing. You yourselves know that these hands of mine have supplied my own needs and the needs of my companions.

—ACTS 20:33-34

After God delivered the Hebrew people from slavery in Egypt, he had Moses lead them through the wilderness for forty years. When they reached the eastern edge of the promised land, Moses delivered two lengthy sermons that basically make up the book of Deuteronomy. Before Moses passed off the scene, he wanted to remind the people not only of God's faithfulness but also of his jealous love for his covenant nation, which was expressed in this strong declaration: "If you ever forget the LORD your God and follow other gods and worship and bow down to them, I testify against you today that you will surely be destroyed. Like the nations that the LORD destroyed before you, so you will be destroyed for not obeying the LORD your God" (Deut. 8:19-20).

Israel was never to worship other gods—in this case, the idols of the Canaanite tribes they would soon conquer. These gods, which were hugely popular and found everywhere throughout the land, included Baal, Ashtoreth, and Molech, among others. God would not accept divided hearts; his people were to worship him alone. The problem wasn't so much that the Israelites would abandon Jehovah altogether, but that they would blend the worship of the true God with elements taken from the worship of these heathen deities. This is called "syncretism."

The practice of syncretism has likewise posed a threat to the Christian church throughout its history, albeit not necessarily because of the influence of idols made of wood and stone. It is often said that Americans worship the god Mammon—money and the material things and pleasures it can buy. No matter how much wealth we have, it's never enough. Jesus made clear that the worship of Mammon was incompatible with serving him: "No one can serve two masters. Either you will hate the one and love the other, or you will be devoted to the one and despise the other. *You cannot serve both God and money*" (Matt. 6:24).

Money and what it brings have a strong seductive power. The apostle Paul cautioned all of us when he said, "Those who want to get rich fall into temptation and a trap and into many foolish and harmful desires that plunge people into ruin and destruction. For the love of money is a root of all kinds of evil. Some people, eager for money, have wandered from the faith and pierced themselves with many griefs" (1 Tim. 6:9–10).

The stories of Christian leaders being seduced by the spirit of greed are tragic. These leaders often start out utterly sincere in their devotion to Christ and with barely two nickels to rub together. Years later they are shells of their former selves because the love of money has robbed them of spiritual power and influence for Christ.

It can happen anywhere, anytime. A pastor has success in

building a large church. The church then supports the pastor generously. Maybe the pastor becomes known outside their church, speaking at conferences, writing books, appearing on television, building a social media following. None of these things is bad in and of itself. By middle age (or sooner), they are able to retire. But they stay where they are, delegating most of the work of the ministry to others, taking their pay and living the good life, but losing the spiritual edge from God that made them such a blessing in past years. Some have even hired others to research and write their sermons, which they then preach as their own. This reminds me of what was said to Andrew Bonar at the beginning of his ministry by an old friend and minister: "Very few men and very few ministers keep up to the end the edge that was on their spirit at the first."[1] This is a tragedy.

Beware the Spirit of Greed

Being free from greed was a qualification for leaders in the early church: "Here is a trustworthy saying: Whoever aspires to be an overseer desires a noble task. Now the overseer is to be above reproach, faithful to his wife, temperate, self-controlled, respectable, hospitable, able to teach, not given to drunkenness, not violent but gentle, not quarrelsome, *not a lover of money*" (1 Tim. 3:1–3).

On this same note, Peter warned the early Christians that "there will be false teachers among you," people who—among other things—would be "experts in greed" (2 Peter 2:1, 14). There are indeed people in our midst today who have an evil genius for swindling innocent people out of their money. One of the most discouraging moments of my life came early in my ministry, at a time when maybe twenty-five people were coming to our church. Most of them were living hand to mouth, and our offerings were pathetically low. A so-called evangelist came to town, rented an auditorium not far from our church, and held a series of meetings. One night he preached about "resurrection power" that, he said, could also provide huge financial blessings. The catch was that you had to pay money to receive the blessing. He offered a choice of $50, $100, and $500 prayer lines! In the front of the auditorium was a coffin. At one point he dramatically threw open the lid of the coffin and a thin young man came flying out using wires connected to him from above the stage. I was told the crowd went wild.

Only the next day did I find out that the young man who had been "resurrected" had started coming to our church about a month before. If that wasn't bad enough, I also learned that an older member of the church had also been at that meeting. He had chosen the $500 line; he paid this swindler $500 for a "blessing"! I can't tell you how discouraged I was since our offerings didn't even total $100. I've often acknowledged that my preaching wasn't very good in those days. (I fell asleep during my sermons, not just the audience.) But honestly, was I doing that poor a job? A young man from my church was helping a con artist scam $500 from another man from my church! I felt like quitting the pastorate just as I was getting started.

The False Prosperity Gospel

But it gets even worse. Unscrupulous preachers have learned that many people are caught up with the spirit of American material-ism and greed, so they develop a message that feeds that greed. Instead of pointing out the modest lifestyles of Jesus and the apostles, they say, "Believe and get rich! Why are you driving a used Toyota? God wants you to have a brand-new Mercedes! If you only have faith . . ."—and, of course, if you send your seed gift to them. A lot of people are eager to hear such a message, and a lot of slick scam artists are only too happy to deliver it to them. Paul said, "I have not coveted anyone's silver or gold or clothing" (Acts 20:33). What a contrast his message was to the nonsense that is regularly spewed from much of religious TV.

It's difficult to understand how people can think the Bible supports the prosperity gospel—the idea that God's plan and purpose for every life includes being wealthy in the here and now. How do believers not see through this, given the clear words of Scripture? Jesus said, "Watch out! Be on your guard against all kinds of greed; life does not consist in an abundance of possessions" (Luke 12:15). Let's also remember Jesus's words to the church in Smyrna, "I know your afflictions and your poverty— yet you are rich!" (Rev. 2:9). In Christ's eyes, real wealth is not measured in dollars.

Of course, at the root of this "religious industry" is the biblical illiteracy of too many believers who can't discern truth from error. Hopefully, none of us are into such deceptive greed; but let's warn our folks, since a lot of people are being deceived, and we don't want it to be sheep from our flock.

The Loss of Eternity

When the blessed hope of Christians—the return of Christ and our eternal home in heaven—becomes dim or nonexistent, the lure of money as our sense of security grows stronger. Jesus knew that and directed us to keep our eyes on heaven: "Do not store up for yourselves treasures on earth, where moths and vermin destroy, and where thieves break in and steal. But store up for yourselves treasures in heaven, where moths and vermin do not destroy, and where thieves do not break in and steal" (Matt. 6:19–20).

We as pastors especially need to keep our eyes on eternity, and we should remind our congregations about true eternal wealth, lest the spirit of greed ensnare us all. By the way, when was the last time you heard a solid sermon about heaven and its rewards? Paul said, "If only for this life we have hope in Christ, we are of all people most to be pitied" (1 Cor. 15:19). Our lives on earth are as a split second compared with eternity in heaven with Christ. God, open our eyes to see what really matters!

I think of a woman from our church who was born and raised in Haiti. She didn't know the Lord. She was raised in a land of crushing poverty dominated by voodoo. When she surrendered her life to Christ, she said, "God, I'll go anywhere you want me to go—just not back to Haiti." I baptized her during one of our Tuesday night prayer meetings. I remember it because it happened to be a national election night. Four years later, on the next election night, we laid hands on her and sent her off as a missionary—to Haiti. That's where God wanted her to go, and that's where she went. She has served faithfully for decades, leading a church and feeding hundreds of children. My wife and I have great love and respect for who she is and what she does. She may not have treasures on earth, but she is surely storing up for herself treasures in heaven.

Here is a good reminder for all of us: Wealth is not a sign of God's special favor; nor is it a sign of advanced spirituality. On the other hand, not being rich doesn't mean you have no faith. Many billionaires curse God and even deny his existence. And yet they're wealthy beyond imagination. So what does it all mean? When the author of the letter to the Hebrews wrote, "Keep your lives free from the love of money and be content with what you have" (Heb. 13:5), he was speaking to both the rich and the poor. Both the rich and the poor can be greedy, and both can be generous. All of us need to be on guard against the spirit of greed.

The Minister's Livelihood

When Carol and I started in the ministry, we were in a small church in Newark, New Jersey, where I received a small salary. We gave that up when we came to the Brooklyn Tabernacle. When I saw that our first offering totaled eighty-five dollars, I knew I had to get a job outside the church to make ends meet. For more than a year, I coached a local boys' basketball team, and Carol worked in a school cafeteria.

We are far from the only people in ministry who have done this. Paul himself established the pattern: "You yourselves know that these hands of mine have supplied my own needs and the needs of my companions" (Acts 20:34). Indeed, he often spoke of earning his own living, including as a tentmaker (Acts 18:3). He told the Thessalonians, "We were not idle when we were with you, nor did we eat anyone's food without paying for it. On the contrary, we worked night and day, laboring and toiling so that we would not be a burden to any of you. We did this, not because we do not have the right to such help, but in order to offer ourselves as a model for you to imitate" (2 Thess. 3:7–9).

So we see that even the apostle Paul had to be "bivocational" sometimes. It's nothing to be ashamed of. In many instances, it is the only way a minister can engage in evangelism and church-building, even as Paul did. I've seen reports that as many as one-third of all American pastors are bivocational.[2] This is even more the case outside the United States. Some years ago our church sponsored a pastors conference in Trinidad. We were told it was best not to schedule it in the daytime because many pastors wouldn't be able to get away from their jobs. Heeding that wise advice, we had a great time in the evening with hundreds of pastors.

Unfortunately, the catchphrase *follow the money* doesn't

apply only to business and politics. Often it's the reason why some churches are reluctant to do evangelistic outreach or donate to the less fortunate. Too many church boards understand only the financial bottom line and have little faith that God will supply what we need as we reach out in Christ's name. "We can't afford that" is a common response, even when it means curtailing the spread of the gospel beyond the church walls.

But thankfully, not everyone has that mindset. I have a dear friend who went to Argentina as a missionary upon graduating from Bible school. There, he fell in love with the daughter of the founder of a fellowship of churches that stress sacrificial living. After their wedding day, they went directly to the city where they felt the Lord wanted them to plant a church. The only problem was that they had no home or church waiting for them. All they had was the call of God and a deep faith in Jesus.

My friend proceeded to build a primitive hut on an empty lot on the outskirts of the city, using spare pieces of anything he could lay his hands on. The newlyweds' first home had a dirt floor and no indoor plumbing. But converts were made, and the church was established through the gospel of Christ.

Decades later a beautiful building is the home of the congregation begun by the sacrifice of two people who had heaven on their minds rather than money in their pockets. May God give all of us freedom from the grip of money so that we can take steps of faith when God calls us to do so.

Raising Money

All of us, regardless of our specific circumstances, have to raise money from time to time. We all need to take offerings because the church still needs funds to operate. There are bills to be paid, ministries and outreaches to support.

I like to point to myself as a good example of how *not* to approach this area. When I started in the ministry, I had already seen a lot of abuses when it came to raising money. Some ministers would preach for fifteen minutes, but the offering would take an hour, with all kinds of manipulation and gimmicks. So I went too far the other way. I was self-conscious about being in the inner city. I didn't want people saying, "He's after my money. I've barely sat down and he's already got his hand in my pocket." So I would simply announce that Carol was going to play some music while we passed the collection plate.

But I was wrong. The Lord had to deal with me, had to show me that I was short-changing the people because I wasn't teaching them biblical truth about giving. I have to confess that I'm still not particularly good at raising money. I don't know of any formula for doing it. Certainly, we can make too little of it and hurt the church's finances and rob believers from the blessing of giving. Or we can make too much of it so that it distracts from the message we're preaching. In these matters, we need wisdom so we can find the balance needed: "If any of you lacks wisdom, you should ask God, who gives generously to all without finding fault, and it will be given to you" (James 1:5). Of course, wisdom is not automatic for every Christian, including leaders. But if we humbly ask in faith, God will abundantly provide.

I was once invited to speak at another church in our area. It was an evening meeting, and about twenty-five people were there. I gave my message, and the pastor, a man who had been in his church for many years, took up the collection. Afterward, he and I went out for a bite to eat, and he asked me if I had any comments on the service.

"Well," I said, "there *is* one thing. It's about the collection."

He gave me a startled look. "What about the collection?" he asked.

"When you said, 'I know a lot of you are too cheap to give, but . . . ,' maybe that wasn't the best way to go."

"What do you mean?" he snapped.

"It's just that those people were *there*. They came out. They showed up. I can understand if you're frustrated that there weren't more people there and finances are low. But I'm not sure insulting the ones who *were* there is a good way to raise funds."

He didn't seem happy with my comments, so I let the matter drop.

Another time I was attending a meeting—not speaking, just participating—when an enthusiastic minister jumped up and shouted, "Hey, it's offering time! God loves a cheerful giver. So let's get cheerful! Everybody clap!" People clapped. He did a little more cheerleading and then said, "Okay. Now I want all you ladies to hand your purse to the lady next to you. And all you guys, hand your wallet to the guy next to you. And take out of their wallet whatever you think they ought to give."

I couldn't believe my ears. If you did that in Brooklyn, well, it might not work out so well. By the way, if someone else has to take the money out of our wallet, will God really be pleased with the gift?

I've even heard of churches where people's donations from the previous week are posted on a bulletin board in the church lobby. Now, *there's* some real peer pressure. Other churches make it a practice to demand that members provide copies of their W-2 forms so the church can determine whether they're giving 10 percent of their income. Another not-so-subtle pressure tactic.

After honestly presenting the needs facing the church, can't we just pray and trust that God will fulfill his promise? Paul reminded the Christian congregation in Philippi that "my God will meet all your needs according to the riches of his glory in Christ Jesus" (Phil. 4:19). Gimmicks and crafty manipulations grieve the Holy Spirit. And in the long run, they backfire. Discerning Christians will think, "If they trust God, why do they need to be manipulative?" Let's remember that God remains faithful and will meet all our needs.

Beware the Building Program

An area of particular importance for pastors is building programs. It's dangerous when leadership mistakes their own ego-driven plans for the will of God. Faith in what God can do must be combined with discerning God's will and timing for any expansion of facilities. Remember that it's the people's hard-earned money that would be misused if we make a mistake.

I knew of a pastor of a church with an auditorium that seated about a thousand people. They held two services every Sunday, each of which drew about six hundred people. One day he announced that he had a vision for a huge, three-thousand-seat auditorium, which would make their church the largest in town. It would of course cost tons of money, but he was sure God would supply. Based on actual numbers, it was hard to make a case that the church even needed a new building—or an additional service, for that matter. But he pressed on. He constantly recited all the faith promises in the Bible.

A real problem soon became evident. The money wasn't coming in. The people weren't making pledges as he hoped. Now the pastor was in a tough spot. He tried to sell his "vision," but his people weren't buying it. Worse, he had made substantial financial commitments for the church that he couldn't fulfill. The Sunday services became more and more focused on raising money. He badgered the people every Sunday to pledge more. Because of the change of atmosphere, people voted with their feet and started *leaving* the church. This was now a recipe for disaster.

So what did that pastor do? Acknowledge the possibility that he was wrong? No. He announced to the congregation, "If you aren't buying into my vision, if you're not going to support me in this, it means I'm not wanted here. I'll leave this church if you don't trust my leadership." And leave he did. And the church? It went bankrupt and sadly had to close its doors.

Let's not start a building program unless we know God is leading us to do it. And we should seek confirmation from associates and mature believers that we're moving in the right direction. If it's the will of Christ, God will meet our needs. But the Lord never said, "I'm your Mastercard in the sky. Charge whatever you want, and I'll pay the tab." Remember, when God led the Israelites through the desert, they had to follow the cloud; the cloud didn't follow *them*. When God said, "I will give you every place where you set your foot, as I promised Moses" (Josh. 1:3), it applied only as long as they set their feet where he told them to go.

The well-known phrase *if you build it, they will come* doesn't work for Christian churches. Sinners don't repent and come to Christ because they're awed by the splendor of a building. It's better to meet in a basement and stay faithful to God in preaching the gospel. Our egos can get us into a lot of trouble. But God always honors the humility it takes to surrender to his will.

The Bottom Line

The bottom line is that in money matters, we must always look to God for guidance and wisdom. Unfortunately, financial pressures in the ministry often cause pastors to rely more on people than God and to look elsewhere for the supply needed. It's tempting to become preoccupied with those who might be able to help the church in a crunch.

Once, during a period when our church was in real financial need, a dear friend who was a successful businessman called to tell me he would bring a guest to the next Sunday service. The guest happened to be worth hundreds of millions of dollars. During the opening worship, I couldn't help but notice that the guest seemed to be enjoying the service and singing along with the congregation. The thought crossed my mind that with one stroke of a pen, this brother could easily provide everything we needed. What was for us a huge amount of money was pocket change to him.

Suddenly I felt the Holy Spirit speaking directly to my heart. I was being chastened: "Are you looking to a *man* instead of me? Look back over all the years. Haven't I always supplied whatever you've needed? And now you're looking to a wealthy man?" I felt the Lord's displeasure deep in my soul. I broke down in tears and repented of my unbelief. Ironically, the offering for the service was less than usual. But I learned an invaluable lesson: I'll never look to anyone but God for the needs of our church. Not to any organization, not to any donor, not to any benefactor. If God chooses to use someone like that, fine. But I'll leave that decision to him. We have to keep our eyes on God alone.

Wait on God

Our church has never hired professional fundraisers, but God has met our needs again and again. I am reminded of one particular time when our backs were against the wall. I have shared this story of God's faithfulness before, but it bears repeating here. My prayer is that it will encourage some pastor whose church may be struggling with a financial challenge that seems insurmountable.

There was a time when we had to add a fourth service to our Sunday schedule to accommodate all the people who were attending. We were thankful that the Lord was adding to our number—especially new believers in Christ—but the growth meant our leadership had to think about the possibility of a new church campus. After much prayer and seeking the counsel of other leaders we respect and who love our church, we searched and found a nearly four-thousand-seat theater that was built in 1918 and is in the heart of downtown Brooklyn.

God miraculously provided, and we were able to purchase the building. But we then learned that the scope of the renovation was huge because the building was in terrible disrepair, with water damage and a host of other problems. To restore it properly called for many millions of dollars. That's a large sum of money, especially for an inner-city church.

Although the situation was challenging, the Lord continued to help us through the regular giving of the congregation and special offerings from friends around the country. A Christian organization also approached us and offered to lend us money. After seeking God's leading, we accepted the loan so that the construction could proceed as quickly as possible. Plans were drawn up and filed with New York City's building department, and the long renovation process began.

Not long after, though, on a Friday afternoon, I received a disturbing call from an official of the institution that was lending us the money. Evidently a mistake had been made in the calculations, and the official was alerting me to a serious problem. He said, "We've been crunching the numbers for phase one of your project. I hate to break it to you, but even with our loan, you still have a shortfall of six million dollars."

"How could that be?" I asked. "Our staff met with your people, and I thought everything had been figured out. What you're really saying is that we'll have to leave our present building, but we can't move into the new building because of the shortfall. So where does that leave us?" He answered, "That's exactly what I'm saying. You need six million dollars, or you can't finish phase one of the project. So how are you going to get it?"

I had no answer but reminded him that when his organization had approached us and offered to help, we made it clear that we were walking by faith. I assured him that we would continue to pray as a church and believe God for the needed funds. The man replied, "Oh, you're trusting God? That's good. *But how are you going to get the money?*"

I knew it was pointless to continue the discussion. I replied that I would be away for about ten days and that I would address the situation when I returned. It was a discouraging phone call, to say the least.

On the following Sunday evening, I left with Carol and a small mission team to minister to hundreds of pastors in Argentina, many of whom lived in impoverished conditions and would be traveling long distances to be with us. On top of the travel expenses, we had also offered to treat the pastors to a luncheon at the end of our time with them. But I wondered, "Why am I taking a trip to bless poor pastors of Argentina when I have this huge sum of money we have to come up with?"

At the end of my time in Argentina, the $6 million figure really got my attention. I thought, "Where am I going to get a sum like that? There's no way our congregation can come up with six million dollars. What if we can't complete the project? Will it be a stumbling block for those who think the Lord wasn't able to help us?"

Perplexed and anxious, I took a long walk one afternoon to pray. At first I thought about the appeal letters I should be writing and the calls I should be making to try to raise the funds we needed. But I didn't even know where to begin. I finally broke down and wept. I prayed, "God, you led us to begin this project.

We just want to provide an adequate space for your people to worship and to be able to bring in others to hear the gospel." After hours of walking and praying, I sensed God speaking to my heart. "Leave it with me," he seemed to say. "Don't worry. Just trust and wait." I soon felt a deep sense of peace.

A few days later, we flew back to New York City on an overnight flight from Buenos Aires. I rested a few hours at home, then went to the church. My desk was piled high with mail and phone messages. I started working through the pile. Around noon I opened a letter from a man in Chicago whom I had met only once or twice in passing. His note said God had impressed him to give us $1 million for the new campus project. Ten minutes later I opened a second letter from the head of a foundation whom I had never met and still have not met to this day. The letter said they were giving us $5 million. Both gifts were unsolicited and totaled the exact amount we needed! The Lord clearly had not forgotten us while we were busy doing his work in South America. Nor had he forgotten the rest of the congregation praying back home.

The Lord helped us just as he promised. And we learned a valuable lesson. When God's people believe and pray, the Lord will provide. But we have to learn to wait on him with faithful, obedient hearts until the answer comes.

> Since ancient times no one has heard,
>> no ear has perceived,
> no eye has seen any God besides you,
>> who acts on behalf of those who wait for him.
> (Isa. 64:4)

What lesson of faith is God seeking to teach you or the church you serve? Are you willing to trust him with that mountain of difficulty you are facing today? Remember that the Lord will never leave you nor forsake you, no matter how hopeless things may seem.

> The LORD longs to be gracious to you;
>> therefore he will rise up to show you
>> compassion.
> For the LORD is a God of justice.
>> Blessed are all who wait for him! (Isa. 30:18)

CHAPTER 12

THE APOSTOLIC PRIORITY

"Now I commit you to God and to the word of his
grace, which can build you up and give you an
inheritance among all those who are sanctified."
When Paul had finished speaking, he knelt
down with all of them and prayed.

—ACTS 20:32, 36

Pastors and leaders need to understand, clearly and definitely, what their priorities are. Sometimes we're so busy with the urgent tasks that we push aside the important ones. But we need to focus our time and energy on what absolutely, positively must be done if we're to minister to people the way God wants us to. Interruptions will happen, and we must stay open to the Holy Spirit, but it's wise to have a sense of what matters most.

Prayer and the Word

One of the most important days in the life of the early church took place early on, even before Saul of Tarsus met Jesus and became Paul the Apostle. Here is how Luke described it:

In those days when the number of disciples was increasing, the Hellenistic Jews among them complained against the Hebraic Jews because their widows were being overlooked in the daily distribution of food. So the Twelve gathered all the disciples together and said, "It would not be right for us to neglect the ministry of the word of God in order to wait on tables. Brothers and sisters, choose seven men from among you who are known to be full of the Spirit and wisdom. We will turn this responsibility over to them and will give our attention to prayer and the ministry of the word." (Acts 6:1–4)

This was a critical moment in the development of the church, and it came about because of a simple problem. The church had undertaken to support the widows in their midst by providing them with food. The Jewish members of the church who had adopted the Greek language and culture felt that their widows weren't being treated as generously as the Jewish widows who had retained the Hebrew language and culture.

On its face, it seems like a simple, practical problem, one for which the apostles devised a simple, practical solution: they would select seven trustworthy individuals to handle the daily food distribution and to make sure it was done fairly. Many commentators think this is where the office of "deacon" began.

But the incident had a much deeper significance. Note that because the apostles thought it was important that they not neglect their calling, they delegated the "waiting on tables" to others so that they could give their full attention to "prayer and the ministry of the word." That established the apostolic priority once and for all. They recognized the crucial importance of dedicating themselves to communion with God and to the Word. Of course, there were no New Testament texts in existence at this time. So this likely involved studying the

Hebrew Scriptures to show how prophecies about Christ had been fulfilled. They also shared the verbal teachings of Jesus, which they had heard with their own ears. This was called the "apostles' teaching" (Acts 2:42). Those early leaders didn't let anything distract them from the Word and prayer. And what was the result of their keeping first things first? "The word of God spread. The number of disciples in Jerusalem increased rapidly, and a large number of priests became obedient to the faith" (Acts 6:7).

Reverse Evangelism

Don't you think we've largely lost this priority in the church today? Pastors have become more CEOs, CFOs, building managers, marketing experts, social media stars—anything but servants of the Lord dedicated first and foremost to prayer and the Word. The result has been loss of vitality, even loss of the church's basic identity. We have in many places ceased to be "the light of the world" and "the salt of the earth" (Matt. 5:13–14) that Jesus called us to be, and this is reflected in the ever-increasing moral decline in both the church and the culture.

When pastors' lives aren't characterized by deep study of the Word and spending time with God, the result is usually reverse evangelism: the world invades and converts the church rather than the church invading and converting the world. I would venture to say that's what's happening to many of the churches in America today. We're not changing the world; the world is changing us. Much of the constant appeal to "stay relevant" is in reality the substitution of carnal ideas for God's spiritual plan for building his church. This trend shows a lack of faith in God's power. Some are more interested in building up their Twitter following than spending time with God.

Many pastors and ministers today are discouraged and burned-out, maybe even ready to quit, because their energy has been depleted, and their effectiveness blunted. But maybe we're burning out unnecessarily because we've departed from the priorities of the early church—from giving ourselves to prayer and the Word. We don't have the endurance we should have, not because the circumstances are so overwhelming but because we don't have the fullness of grace that God wants to give us.

Under the best of circumstances, the ministry is difficult. There are hardships, obstacles, satanic attacks. This was true in the early church, and it's been true ever since. The greatest men and women of God have all been attacked and had difficult moments, strains, and stresses of all kinds. But they've overcome. How? Not because of something innate in them but because they spent time with God daily to receive fresh, supernatural grace.

The apostle Peter probably led the way in delegating to others the feeding of widows because he so well remembered what happened in the garden of Gethsemane. Instead of watching quietly in prayer as Jesus directed, Peter had fallen asleep. "'Couldn't you . . . keep watch with me for one hour?' [Jesus] asked Peter. 'Watch and pray so that you will not fall into temptation. The spirit is willing, but the flesh is weak'" (Matt. 26:40–41). That failure of faith wasn't going to happen again if Peter could help it. He and the other leaders knew their priorities—be with God and then preach. And then do it all over again.

Then = Now

Could it be that because these early leaders devoted themselves to God's priorities—prayer, the Word, preaching the gospel—the Lord's blessing was upon them and he "added to their number daily those who were being saved" (Acts 2:47)?

Remember that nearly all the apostles were fishermen by trade, and all were spiritual failures who had denied the Lord and fled on the night he was arrested. Now they were building the Christian church! Their ability to do so was because of God's grace, not because of something they were doing in their own strength. Search all of church history and you won't find a man or woman who was used mightily by God who wasn't also a person of prayer and the Word. They were human, with weaknesses and faults, to be sure. But they found strength in being with God.

To Be with Him

When Jesus called his first disciples, he "went up on a mountainside and called to him those he wanted, and they came to him. He appointed twelve that they might be with him and that he might send them out to preach and to have authority to drive out demons" (Mark 3:13–15). Notice the first thing that the twelve were called to do. Not to write a book. Not to build a building. Not to raise money. *Not even to preach.* He called them that they might *be with him.* Effective ministry would flow from communion, or intimate fellowship, with Jesus.

Intimate fellowship is deeper than mere relationship. There are many kinds of relationships people can have: family relationships, friendships, acquaintances, romantic relationships, work relationships, and more. But even blood relations don't always have intimate fellowship with one another. The same is true for believers. All true Christians have a personal relationship with the Lord. We become members of God's family. But we are called to more. "We proclaim to you what we have seen and heard, so that you also may have *fellowship* with us. And our *fellowship* is with the Father and with his Son, Jesus Christ. We write this to make our joy complete" (1 John 1:3–4).

John was writing to believers who already had a relationship with Christ. But his goal was to draw them into something more—fellowship with Christ. Communion with the Lord is our first and highest calling.

Does that sound outdated? Don't believe anyone who subscribes to a new way of doing ministry that does away with our first calling to be with the Lord. The top priority for the first apostles is still the top priority for you and for me: *we must spend time with him.*

Our First Calling

This message about our first calling in life has continually inspired me and led to one of the most precious moments I've had in the ministry.

Years ago I was preaching this message at a gathering of pastors at the Billy Graham Training Center at the Cove in Asheville, North Carolina. Hundreds of ministers were present. And there in the front row was Will Graham, Billy Graham's grandson, who has a preaching ministry of his own. He had just been named director of the Cove, a conference and retreat center that is visited year-round by believers from around the country. As I was speaking, I noticed that Will was taking notes. It was gratifying to think I might be saying something that encouraged my fellow minister and brother in Christ.

The next day I was doing a book signing for one of my books at the Cove bookstore when Will rushed in and brought the activities to a halt. "You have to come with me now, Pastor Jim. Let's go!" I resisted, pointing to the folks still in line. But he insisted and said to the people, "He'll sign your book later. But he has to go with me now!" So I left with him, feeling bad about the people left waiting.

As we got into Will's car, I asked, "Where are we going?" He replied, "My father wants you to meet my grandfather, and my grandfather agrees. You've represented our organization with pastors in Ottawa, Buffalo, and Green Bay; and yet you've never met Billy Graham!"

My wife, Carol, had already had that privilege multiple times. First, because the Brooklyn Tabernacle Choir had sung at one of Billy Graham's evangelistic meetings years before in Philadelphia; then on another memorable day in Central Park, where attendance records were broken, making the meeting the largest single evangelistic rally in North American history; and finally, during his last meeting before he retired, which took place at Flushing Meadows Corona Park in New York City and also drew hundreds of thousands of people. But I had never met him.

So there we were driving up to Billy Graham's modest home. I felt uncomfortable and said to Will, "I really don't want to bother your grandfather." We're talking about the world-renowned evangelist who had visited nearly every country in the world before he retired and had such a profound impact on people, including US presidents and other world leaders. He was in his nineties at the time. I knew he had lost his wife, and I had just read somewhere that he was recovering from some bronchial problems. I thought it might not be a good time, and I didn't want to intrude. But Will insisted: "No, you have to meet him. This is important."

When we arrived at the house, there was Billy Graham, sitting in a wheelchair, with hair white as snow and sunglasses on. I noticed the tubes that helped oxygen flow into his ailing lungs. As I was led forward to greet him, I felt nervous and a bit ill at ease. Will introduced me, and Billy Graham lifted his head to greet me. "Hello, Dr. Graham," I responded. "I'm happy to meet you." He had difficulty hearing, so Will stood close to him and raised his voice: "Grandpa Bill, Pastor Cymbala has represented us at pastors' meetings we've done for the Billy Graham Association. He's here at the Cove, and he preached a message last night that really blessed me." Dr. Graham lifted his head again—I still couldn't see his eyes because of the sunglasses—and he asked, "What was his message?" Will filled him in on what I had spoken about.

What a surreal moment that was for me! Here was Will Graham telling his grandfather, the legendary preacher of the gospel, about a sermon by Jim Cymbala, a nobody! When I started in the ministry, I never would have thought such a moment could ever happen.

Will went on: "Grandpa Bill, Pastor Jim preached from Mark chapter three about our first calling in life. He reminded us that our first calling, especially as pastors, is not to be CEOs or CFOs or building managers or even preachers or teachers. No matter how busy we are, even doing the work of the Lord, we can't lose sight of that first calling."

At that, Dr. Graham asked in a frail voice, "And what *is* that calling?" Will replied, "Grandpa Bill, Pastor Jim said that the first call is to be with the Lord. *Then* go out and preach and have authority over evil spirits. But first we have to *be* with him. And from that fellowship and communion with the Lord, everything else will flow. And you know, Grandpa, I have so much on my plate. I needed to hear that because we can start running around and miss out on being with Jesus." Suddenly Billy Graham lifted his head again and in a broken voice said, "No, *I* needed to hear that. Because I'm ninety-six years old, and I need to be with Jesus more."

When he said that, tears came to my eyes. I was taken aback by his sincerity and, especially, by his humility. It was Billy Graham speaking—the premier evangelist of the twentieth century, used by God around the world. And what was he saying?

Not "Oh, I already know that. I didn't need him to remind me." Instead, he was saying, "No, that was for me."

I never said another word to Dr. Graham except goodbye. I've always treasured that moment because the message had touched someone I really admired. If we spend more time in communion with God, there's no telling what inspiration, what direction, or what new power from the Holy Spirit we will discover.

A Spiritual Revival

There is both a need and an opportunity for leaders who will pursue the apostolic priority of spending time with God in prayer and in his Word. There is a remnant of God's people, from all around the country, who long for preaching from the whole Bible and who want to go to a house of prayer, to a service that is guided by the Holy Spirit, where they can leave saying, "God is really among you!" (1 Cor. 14:25). In other words, serious believers desire to witness a true spiritual revival.

Let's return to a moment before the apostle Paul was converted, to the day when the Christian church was born. After Jesus resurrected from the dead, he spent forty days appearing off and on to his disciples. During those times together, he spoke about the kingdom of God. The disciples were sure now that he was alive from the dead. They had begun to understand the meaning of his death and resurrection. The world around them, although hostile, desperately needed to hear the message so they could believe and experience salvation. And yet the risen Lord told them to wait in Jerusalem for the promise he had spoken of previously.

On one occasion, while he was eating with them, he gave them this command: "Do not leave Jerusalem, but wait for the gift my Father promised, which you have heard me speak about. For John baptized with water, but in a few days you will be baptized with the Holy Spirit."

. . . He said to them: "It is not for you to know the times or dates the Father has set by his own authority. But you will receive power when the Holy Spirit comes on you; and you will be my witnesses in Jerusalem, and in all Judea and Samaria, and to the ends of the earth." (Acts 1:4–5, 7–8)

Jesus was saying that although the disciples may have comprehended the message of salvation, they still needed to receive the power that only the Holy Spirit would impart as he came upon them. They needed both the correct message and the power of God to effectively witness for Jesus.

After Christ's ascension, the disciples returned to Jerusalem, where they used an upper room as their meeting place for ten days. They probably gathered numerous times as they waited for the promised Holy Spirit. Here's what happened then: "When the day of Pentecost came, they were all together in one place. Suddenly a sound like the blowing of a violent wind came from heaven and filled the whole house where they were sitting. They saw what seemed to be tongues of fire that separated and came to rest on each of them. All of them were filled with the Holy Spirit and began to speak in other tongues as the Spirit enabled them" (Acts 2:1–4).

I want to distill this memorable moment when the church was born to one main fact. Yes, about 120 believers were unified in one place. Yes, what seemed like tongues of fire rested on each of them. Yes, they all spoke in other tongues as the Spirit enabled them. But I want to draw your attention to the fact that a sound of a mighty wind *came from heaven*. The blessing, the fulfillment of the promise Jesus made, the manifestations that ensued—it all happened because *something came from heaven*. It wasn't man-made. It was something supernatural from God. The Christian church was born not by human effort, talent or intellect; it gained its impetus from Almighty God. Peter's sermon that followed, and the resulting harvest of three thousand converts, all began with God sending *something from heaven*.

Can we not all agree on this fact? Every church in America needs a fresh infusion of what gave birth to the Christian church in the first place—*something from heaven*.

We want God to fan the flame in our hearts and in our churches—but that is a flame *he* must light, not something you or I can manufacture. Yet we must do our part and respond to God's promises. Listen to what it says in his Word: "Come near to God and he will come near to you" (James 4:8). When will he come near to us with holy fire and strength? When we first come near to him! When will we receive something from heaven? When we ask! (Matt. 7:7). There is not one promise we can claim until we refuse to accept *what is* and reach out in repentance, humility, and faith for what *could be*, through the Holy Spirit's fire burning among us. What will it look like? We don't need to understand or predict that. Why don't we just leave it with God as we trust his faithfulness?

The Question

We're all at a fork in the road and have to choose. Do we want to be like the apostles and the other men and women in the upper room, who were used to build the church of Jesus Christ? Or do we want an endless procession of passing fads? Another new gimmick, another new "vision," another new manifestation, replaced by another and another and another?

If we wait on the Lord to help us, do you think he'll ignore us? It was he who made the promise, and he wants to give us more than we can ask or even imagine. But the question for all of us is, What do we really want? And are we prepared to wait before the Lord to receive it?

Epilogue

Throughout this book we've been studying Paul's last remarks to the Ephesian elders. But what does all this look like on the ground—with real ministry to real people? In an earlier part of the book of Acts, Peter and John were heading to the temple to pray. They providentially encountered one man who was lame, out of the many needy people who had made it a practice "to beg from those going into the temple courts" (Acts 3:2). The man "was being carried to the temple gate called Beautiful" while Peter and John were making their way there (Acts 3:2).

When the man asked them for money, the Holy Spirit must have revealed to Peter that God was about to do something extraordinary. But why only *this* man on *that* day with so much other need around them? Peter knew well enough that God's ways are past finding out and that it was his duty to respond to the Holy Spirit's leading right then and there.

The lack of finances, common to the early church, is highlighted by Peter's response: "Silver or gold I do not have" (Acts 3:6). That poor beggar was about to receive something far better than a handout. Peter invoked the powerful name of Jesus as he commanded the lame man: "Walk!" The miracle that ensued and the man's excited walking and jumping and vocal praising of God eventually drew a crowd. Peter quickly realized God had opened an unexpected door to share the gospel message (Acts 3:11–26).

Peter boldly gave the message and concluded his remarks with the promise that "when God raised up his servant [Jesus], he sent him first to you to bless you by turning each of you from your wicked ways" (Acts 3:26). We're talking about some bold gospel preaching here, folks.

Not surprisingly, the religious authorities didn't appreciate the miracle nor Peter's "proclaiming in Jesus the resurrection of the dead" (Acts 4:2). They went further by seizing Peter and John and tossing them into jail for the night. Once again we are reminded that preaching the true gospel doesn't always result in popularity or a large honorarium. As with Peter and John, it could result in opposition and trouble. But although Peter and John were put in prison, the enemies of Christ couldn't hinder the fact that "many who heard the message believed; so the number of men who believed grew to about five thousand" (Acts 4:4). Wow! One simple gospel message by a former fisherman, helped by the Holy Spirit, produced an amazing harvest. And that same gospel has never lost its power.

In the morning, Peter and John were hauled before the council of Jewish rulers, elders, and teachers of the law, who asked them, "By what power or what name did you do this?" (Acts 4:7). What happened next has valuable lessons for us. Acts 4:8 notes that "Peter, filled with the Holy Spirit," boldly responded to the hostile authorities. What was the significance of relating that Peter was filled with the Spirit? Most likely there was an impartation of special grace from God for the challenge before Peter. Can we not gain something for our own lives from this testimony of God's faithfulness?

Peter continued, "It is by the name of Jesus Christ of Nazareth, whom you crucified but whom God raised from the dead, that this man stands before you healed" (Acts 4:10). Peter's response resulted in threats from the religious authorities. But think about this: If the apostles had instead promised to restrict their preaching only to the lives of Abraham and Moses, the council would have been pacified. If they had pledged to do a twelve-week expository series from the book of Nehemiah, without mention of the name of Jesus, they would likely have been commended. They would have even been given permission to pray in the name of Almighty God, the Great I Am, or the Holy One—anything but the name of Jesus Christ, our Savior!

That was two thousand years ago. And still today the name of Jesus is a stumbling block. Yet if we cease glorifying, preaching about, and praying in the name of Jesus, it means we've given in to the same antichrist spirit that opposed Peter and John. It is disheartening that more and more sermons hardly mention Jesus. He alone is the exact image of the invisible God. So why wouldn't we focus on him? Any other picture of God is of Satan. "Salvation is found in no one else, for there is no other name under heaven given to mankind by which we must be saved" (Acts 4:12). Call it narrow or antiquated—call it anything you like—but that is God's only way to forgive sin and grant eternal life.

The conclusion of the apostles' defense highlights the difference between their bold proclamation and the cautious, people-pleasing preaching so prevalent around us. Peter and John weren't afraid of how their audiences might react. They told them the truth in love, even though it could cost them their lives.

Remember that less than six months before, these two men had deserted Jesus on the night he was arrested. But now they were filled with boldness through the Holy Spirit. "When [the members of the council] saw the courage of Peter and John and realized that they were unschooled, ordinary men, they were astonished and they took note that these men had been with Jesus" (Acts 4:13). But what could they say about what had taken place, since the formerly lame man was standing there with Peter and John?

Notice how unbelief can harden the human heart. Although the religious authorities couldn't deny that the apostles had performed a "notable sign," they decided that they must "stop this thing from spreading any further among the people" (Acts 4:16–17). The religious leaders weren't interested in truth; they were concerned only with keeping their leadership position with its perks and privileges. After warning Peter and John "to speak no longer to anyone in this name" (Acts 4:17) and threatening them, they let them go. This historical episode was the first persecution of the Christian church.

So where do you think Peter and John went? To Pontius Pilate, in the halls of government, to protest such unfair treatment? To complain to the media about the violation of their right to worship? Or, more realistically, did they get out of town ASAP to avoid danger? No, they went back to where other believers were gathered and reported all the threats made against them. And that started a prayer meeting!

Hadn't God said, "Call on me in the day of trouble [and] I will deliver you" (Ps. 50:15)? Hadn't Jesus taught, "Ask and it will be given to you" (Matt. 7:7)? Peter and John had their priorities right. What was needed at that moment was not a Bible conference, a time of praise and worship, or a teaching series on the mark of the beast. "There's a time for everything, and a season for every activity under the heavens" (Eccl. 3:1), but at that moment the only thing to do was pray fervently. And fervently pray they did. "When they heard this, they raised their voices together in [loud, vocal] prayer to God" (Acts 4:24).

Although vocal congregational prayer is found in Scripture, it has gone out of style or even become forbidden in some circles. But it was the normal New Testament response to the dangerous circumstances that those early believers faced. The whole world, including both gentiles and Jews, was gathered against them, with no protection to be found. Only hostility and threats. But the moment their united cry went up to God, they could not be defeated.

Remember their prayer: "Now, Lord, consider their threats and enable your servants to speak your word with great boldness. Stretch out your hand to heal and perform signs and wonders through the name of your holy servant Jesus" (Acts 4:29–30). Notice the two requests made to God:

1. They asked for divine grace to spread the gospel message of Jesus with "great boldness." They understood all too well how easily intimidation could silence or compromise the message that needed to be proclaimed. Even though the apostles had been incredibly bold that same day before the council, they knew that only the Holy Spirit could continually impart the boldness they needed.
2. As they pledged to spread the message of Christ, they asked God to work with them and confirm the word supernaturally with "signs and wonders," all done "through the name of your holy servant Jesus."

Should we not follow that model of prayer in our churches today? Aren't we surrounded by a hostile culture, a complicit media, and an educational system that rejects God and threatens to brainwash children against all that God says is right? Who can help us boldly share Jesus except the God of heaven? If Christians don't lift their voices in prayer, how can we expect to overcome spiritual opposition and successfully follow in the footsteps of the apostles?

The account in Acts concludes, "The place where they were meeting was shaken" (Acts 4:31). The result? Instead of cowering in fear, the believers spoke the word of God boldly. Think of the power that's still available as we give ourselves totally to Jesus Christ. Isn't the Lord enough? Of course he is!

The New Testament and church history are filled with countless examples of spiritual revivals casting light into the surrounding darkness, bringing multitudes into the kingdom of Christ. No power on earth can stop us from being a blessing by announcing the good news of Jesus and his love. And who has God constantly used to accomplish this? Common, ordinary people like you and me. Frail and faulty we may be, but his power is made perfect in our weakness (2 Cor. 12:9).

Hold on, my friend, to your calling from God. Rely on his faithfulness to finish the work he has begun in your ministry and church. To all who trust his Word, his promises remain the same. The best is yet to come.

DISCUSSION QUESTIONS

These discussion questions are provided for individuals or groups that wish to read and further discuss the content of the book. Each session matches a chapter of the book for a reading group, but they can also be used together with the (sold separately). If you plan to utilize the video study with these questions, we recommend having each participant in the study read the chapter associated with that session before you gather. Begin your meeting time with prayer and then introduce the topic of the session. Watch the video sessions together as a group and then take time to discuss several of the questions provided in this section. You do not need to work through every question provided. Choose which questions best match the interests of your group and the time you have available. Close each session with a time of personal reflection and prayer as a group.

Each person in the group should have his or her own copy of the book and a Bible. To get the most out of your group experience, keep the following points in mind. First, the real growth in this study will happen during your small group time. This is where you will process the content of the teaching for the week, ask questions, and learn from others as you hear what God is doing in their lives. For this reason, it is important for you to be fully committed to the group and attend each session so you can build trust and rapport with the other members. If you choose to only go through the motions, or if you refrain from participating, there is a lesser chance you will find what you're looking for during this study.

Second, remember the goal of your small group is to serve as a place where people can share, learn about God, and build intimacy and friendship. For this reason, seek to make your group a safe place. This means being honest about your thoughts and feelings and listening carefully to everyone else's opinion.

Third, resist the temptation to fix a problem someone might be having or to correct his or her theology, as that's not the purpose of your small group time. Also, keep everything your group shares confidential. This will foster a rewarding sense of community in your group and create a place where people can heal, be challenged, and grow spiritually.

Keep in mind that the discussion questions are simply meant to kick-start your thoughts so you are both open to what God wants you to hear and also how to apply it to your life. As you go through this study, be open and listen to what God is saying to you.

Note: If you are a group leader, keep the following guidelines in mind.

Group Size: While these discussion questions can be used by individuals for self-reflection, they are designed to be experienced in a group setting such as a Bible study, Sunday school class, or any small group gathering. To ensure everyone has enough time to participate in discussions, it is recommended that large groups of more than eight people break up into smaller groups of four to six people each.

Timing: Each session will take approximately ninety minutes. For those who have less time to meet, you can use fewer questions.

Facilitation: If you watch the videos, each group should

appoint a facilitator who is responsible for starting the video and keeping track of time during discussions and activities. Facilitators may also read questions aloud and monitor discussions, prompting participants to respond and assuring that everyone has the opportunity to participate.

Chapter 1: A Tale of Two Departures

1. According to Pastor Cymbala, what significant changes were made in the church life that began to negatively affect Matt and Sarah's walk with Christ? (What's Going On Here?)

2. How can people who are truly called to pastoral ministry get discouraged and think of departing from ministry altogether? (Discouraged, Disheartened, All but Defeated)

3. Why are fundamentals important to return to when one is facing a rut in life or particularly ministry and what are the fundamentals for Christians? (Who's Leaving Whom?)

4. How might tradition become a dangerous detour for Christian faithfulness? Provide your own example if you can think of one. (Beware of Detours)

5. How can Christians properly use tradition for Christian faithfulness? Provide an example where it can be done well. (Beware of Detours)

6. How might following the latest trends become a dangerous detour for Christian faithfulness? Provide an example if you can. (Beware of Detours)

7. How can Christians properly use the latest trends for Christian faithfulness? Provide an example where it can be done well. (Beware of Detours)

8. How have you seen politics become a dangerous detour for Christian faithfulness? (Beware of Detours)
9. Explain how culture can become a dangerous detour for Christian faithfulness and provide your own example. (Beware of Detours)
10. Why is it significant that Paul begins his farewell speech to the Ephesian elders by reminding them of his personal life and conduct among them? (Do As You Have Seen Me Do)

Chapter 2: The Heart of Ministry

1. Why is the image of a "bondservant" an important biblical image for ministers? (The Heart of Ministry)
2. Why does the spiritual condition of a church tend to reflect the spiritual leadership of the church? How ought this motivate ministers of the gospel? (Leadership Is Crucial)
3. Why can ministers have confidence that God will provide the resources of heaven to them? What should their perspective be when they feel helpless in themselves? (Leadership Is Crucial)
4. Why is it tempting to rely on programs rather than people for building up God's kingdom? (People, Not Programs)
5. What quality does God look for most when raising up ministers and why? How do the disciples prove this is the case biblically? (People, Not Programs)
6. What are common definitions of humility you have heard? What is true humility? (True Humility)
7. How is Jesus the perfect picture of true humility? What should be our response to our natural tendency for self-aggrandizement? (True Humility)

8. Why do people think ministers are the equivalent of CEOs or CFOs? What is wrong with the image? (The Weeping Pastor)

9. Why are many ministers and leaders taught they should not get close to their flocks? What is a better perspective on relating to congregants? (The Weeping Pastor)

10. What are temptations you struggle with in being open to ministry opportunities? How can you grow in humility to be ready for such opportunities? (The Story of David)

Chapter 3: Through Many Dangers, Toils, and Snares

1. What are some challenging testimonies you have heard, read, or experienced that reinforced the dangers of gospel ministry? (Through Many Dangers, Toils, and Snares)

2. Why is it significant that Paul and Jesus engaged in their ministries knowing there were enemies who wanted them dead? How can we find encouragement by their witness? (Severe Testing)

3. How do trouble and adversity demonstrate God's power? Why does this actually help our ministries? (A Treasure in Jars of Clay)

4. Why is it tempting to think challenges and oppositions to our ministries are signs of faithlessness? How can it mean the opposite from a biblical perspective? (A Treasure in Jars of Clay)

5. What would you say are the most common discouragements in ministry? How can they lead to pastoral burn out? (Recapturing Our Calling)

6. How does Elijah provide an example of God's nourishing of a discouraged servant? What can we learn for our own discouragements? (Recapturing Our Calling)

7. What lesson does God teach his people with the provision of manna in the wilderness? What are practical ways we can live day by day in ministry? (Renewed Day by Day)

8. Why is it tempting to get stuck either lamenting what we did not do in the past, or becoming focused on what is the future? Why is today a vital concept for ministry? (Today Is Everything)

9. In addition to yourself, who else in your life and ministry would be affected by your inability to be spiritually nourished? What are practical steps you can take to be *daily* refilled in the Lord? (Daily Refill)

10. How does a vision for the future of our Christian hope motivate our own life and ministry today? (Living in the Future, Living in the Invisible)

Chapter 4: Not Ashamed of the Gospel

1. Explain where the Great Commission is found in Scripture and what it means for the church today. (One Soul at a Time)

2. Why does Jesus say workers are needed for the fields of harvest as it relates to the gospel? How should this motivate our own ministries? (Look at the Fields)

3. What is the place of ordinary believers in proclaiming the gospel? How can they be encouraged in that task? (Look at the Fields)

4. How is the work of a pastor different than that of a life coach? How does Paul exemplify this? (Preaching for Conversions)

5. Why is it important for ministers' Old Testament sermons to reveal Christ to their listeners? (Learning from the Sermons in Acts)

6. What are some examples you can think of where people are tempted to add to and subtract from the gospel of Jesus Christ? Why is this wrong? (Add Nothing, Subtract Nothing)

7. How can a church leader grow in awareness at the spiritual condition of their flock? Should they assume everyone is a believer that regularly attends? Why or why not? (The Sunday Morning Mission Field)

8. Why is it challenging to preach a sermon that will reach unbelievers and believers alike? How can ministers utilize simplicity in their points to both without being shallow? (Preaching to the Saved?)

9. In what ways are we tempted to be ashamed of the gospel? How can our hearts be encouraged to not be ashamed? (Not Ashamed)

Chapter 5: The Unabridged Bible

1. What truths in Scripture do you find are uncomfortable to preach? How can you resolve yourself to preach the whole counsel of God? ("I Never Held Back")

2. How can a minister faithfully proclaim the heinousness of sin without leaving congregants in a spiral of misery and despair? ("I Never Held Back")

3. How has biblical illiteracy become a vicious cycle that preachers have often exacerbated? (Preach the Word)

4. Why is the image of an "ambassador" an important biblical image for ministers? How can it encourage them in the face of opposition? (Christ's Ambassadors)

5. How should the knowledge that God is always a witness to a minister's preaching motivate their courage in proclaiming the gospel? (Christ's Ambassadors)

6. How does the image of a wise parent or a good physician hold ministers accountable for their preaching? (Wise Parents, Good Physicians)
7. What temptations might prevent a minister from being frank about the hardships of the Christian life? Why is it important that believers be warned about them? (Admonitions and Warnings)
8. How should the eternal destiny of individuals motivate a minister's preaching? (Prophetic Fearlessness)
9. Why should we not expect the Holy Spirit to work where God's Word is not honored and proclaimed faithfully? Won't the Spirit work apart from his Word? Why or why not? (Prophetic Fearlessness)

Chapter 6: Who's In Charge Here?

1. In the church, who is in charge of the church and why?
2. The Holy Spirit is what compelled Paul and his ministry. What do you think it means to be compelled by the Holy Spirit today and how would you know? (Who's In Charge Here?)
3. In what ways has the modern world and especially modern business planning entered the church? Is there anything positive or negative about this? Explain. (Following in Faith)
4. What would it look like for a church to attempt to follow its calling, but to do so without the Holy Spirit? (Following in Faith)
5. Based on your understanding of Scripture, how do you think the Spirit leads the church during worship? (Holy Bedlam)
6. What does it mean to be filled with the Spirit? How

would you explain to a new convert what it means to be filled with the Spirit? (Filled with the Spirit)

7. What does it mean to "grieve" the Holy Spirit? What steps can individuals or churches make who feel they have grieved the Spirit? (Deprived of the Spirit)

8. What does it mean to "quench" the Holy Spirit? Why can even orthodox, Bible-believing churches fall into the error of quenching the Spirit? (Deprived of the Spirit)

9. What does it look like to emphasize the Word to the exclusion of the Spirit? What does it look like to emphasize the Spirit to the exclusion of the Word? (Balancing Word and Spirit)

Chapter 7: Preaching in the Power of the Spirit

1. Why would Paul's boast in preaching apart from eloquence or human wisdom have been strange to his audience? In what ways are we negatively tempted to rely purely on eloquence or human wisdom in preaching? (Preaching in the Power of the Spirit)

2. What temptations are there towards self-exaltation in preaching? What is the proper remedy for this temptation? (Preaching in the Power of the Spirit)

3. What does it look like to preach with a "demonstration of the Spirit's power?" Is that still possible today? Why or why not? (Preaching in the Power of the Spirit)

4. What is the place of deep conviction when preaching? Why can eloquent preaching apart from conviction be stunted in its fruit? (Deep Conviction)

5. What ought a pastor do when they feel they are making no progress in moving people through their preaching? What promises can be anticipated when preaching in reliance upon the Spirit? (Holy Spirit, Help Me!)

6. How would you explain to a new convert what it means that the "Spirit himself intercedes for us through wordless groans" (Romans 8:26–27)? (Praying As We Preach)

7. Why is it tempting to fall into a mechanical and repetitive approach to ministry that does not rely on the Holy Spirit? How can this be avoided? (Praying As We Preach)

8. How can preaching be prophetic without foretelling the future? Why is it important for the church? (Prophetic Preaching)

9. Given the primacy and explicit place of prayer in Scripture, why do you think many churches can become lethargic or uninterested in devoting themselves to prayer? ("Lead My People to Pray")

10. What are some practical steps you can take to encourage prayer in your life and in the life of your church? What challenges will you face in encouraging your church to that end? (Where to Begin)

Chapter 8: Unconditional Surrender

1. Why would a willingness to die for the gospel powerfully impact a person's ministry? (Unconditional Surrender)

2. How does understanding the goal of our redemption impact our personal day-to-day life as Christians? (Or how should it?) (Eyes on Eternity)

3. In what ways should the gospel impact our view towards those who are forsaken or despised in society? In ministering to such, what resolve must a believer have in the face of opposition? (Loving the Forsaken)

4. What does it mean to be "consecrated to God?" How can ordinary believers be encouraged to see their entire lives can be consecrated to God? (Consecrated to God)

5. Is it possible to acquire the power to be a living sacrifice to God by our own effort? Why or why not? (Consecrated to God)

6. What did Jesus mean when he said, "Blessed are the poor in spirit, for theirs is the kingdom of heaven?" How should this impact our outlook on the Christian life? (Blessed Are the Beggars)

7. Why is it important for a minister to both finish their race and complete their task? ("It's Always Too Soon to Quit")

8. How can a pastor secretly give up on their race and task without anyone knowing about it? What would you say to a pastor who was doing that? ("It's Always Too Soon to Quit")

9. What is a general call for believers versus a personal call for them? How can they learn both? (True Success)

10. What are some common views of "success" in the eyes of the world? What does true success look like before God? (True Success)

Chapter 9: Keep Watch

1. Why is the flock of a church at risk if their shepherd is not keeping watch over themselves? (Keep Watch)

2. Can congregants maintain their faith well by receiving the Word only once a week on Sunday? Why or why not? (Feed, Guide, Protect)

3. Will believers grow apart from the Spirit working in them? Why or why not? How can we fall into the temptation of thinking accountability structures will prevent them from sin? (Spiritual Accountability)

4. What lessons can ministers learn from the examples of Judas Iscariot and Demas? (Spiritual Accountability)

5. Why is it important for ministers to acknowledge the hardships Christ promises will come in due time? How ought ministers to respond to this knowledge? (Hardship Is Coming)

6. How can ministers encourage their flock to be aware of hardships and prepare them to encounter the trials they will face? (Hardship Is Coming)

7. What makes false teachers at times challenging to identify? Should ministers engage them in some fashion? Why or why not? (Savage Wolves)

8. How should the fact that Jesus bought the church with his own blood motivate the ministry of ministers? (The Flock God Cherishes)

Chapter 10: Division Is Deadly

1. Why did Jesus's appeal that Satan would not drive out Satan prove an effective response to the Jewish authorities' accusation that Jesus was demonic? (Division Is Deadly)

2. Why does the church suffer when it is divided against itself? (Division Brings Weakness)

3. How can major crises reveal the health of Christian unity within a church? What are some ways believers can respond in love over differences revealed through crises? (Pandemic Pandemonium)

4. How should Christ's death on the cross control our understanding of how we minister to and relate to all people? (The Dark Stain of Racism)

5. What are three or four significant ways we are tempted to emphasize our differences with other Christians rather than our similarities? How can we resist that temptation? (One Lord, One Faith, One Baptism)

6. Why are schisms and divisions worldly according to Paul? How can we grow in accepting other believers who might believe secondary issues differently from us? (Is Christ Divided?)

7. Why is it tempting for pastors to ignore divisions in their church? What dangers will arise if divisions are not addressed? (Division in the Local Church)

8. What are some practical ways a minister can proactively prevent disunity within a church? (Dealing with Division)

9. Do you agree that slander and gossip are the biggest culprits in creating division and strife? Why or why not? How should slander and gossip be handled by believers? (Dealing with Division)

10. What are the dangers in focusing just on a person's giftings and capabilities when looking for leaders? How can the church encourage future leaders to be humble and kind? (Dealing with Division)

Chapter 11: Money

1. Why is the love of money capable of making a Christian syncretistic in their faith? How is this a temptation even for ministers? (Money)

2. How is being an "expert in greed" a sign of a false teacher? What are some signs you have seen of a false teacher clearly exerting this? (Beware the Spirit of Greed)

3. What leads to people being swindled by the prosperity gospel? How can ministers help their own flock with that problem? (The False Prosperity Gospel)

4. Why does losing sight of eternity provide fertile soil for greed? How can ministers maintain that vision of eternity in their own lives and their congregation's lives? (The Loss of Eternity)

5. Do you think a poor person can be greedy? Do you think a rich person can be generous? Why or why not? (The Loss of Eternity)

6. How does Paul's own ministry provide an example of how pastors can sometimes support themselves with other work? What potential benefits can arise from their work in these areas beyond supporting their living? (The Minister's Livelihood)

7. How ought ministers to approach the issue of gathering the offering from believers without being manipulative or faithless in the process? (Raising Money)

8. Why doesn't the concept "if you build it, they will come" work for Christian churches? How can ministers guard their own hearts against such thinking? (Beware the Building Program)

9. How can fear of financial pressure ensnare us to men and grieve the Holy Spirit? (The Bottom Line)

10. In what ways can financial needs provide an opportunity for faith and trust in the Lord? How can believers prayerfully wait on God without being presumptive? (Wait on God)

Chapter 12: The Apostolic Priority

1. What do you think are common priorities felt by ministers that might not be apostolic priorities? Which of them are you most tempted by and how can you overcome those temptations? (The Apostolic Priority)

2. What was the impetus for revealing the apostolic priority for ministers? Why is Acts 6 so crucial for understanding the purpose of the church? (Prayer and the Word)

3. What is reverse evangelism? How should a minister protect themselves and their church from reverse evangelism? (Reverse Evangelism)

4. Why can a misguided placing of priorities lead to pastoral burnout? What is the answer to this? (Reverse Evangelism)

5. How can we see that the apostle's success in spreading the gospel was not by their own strength? Why should ministers today be marked similarly? (Then = Now)

6. What is the first priority for every believer? Why is this so important? (To Be with Him)

7. What is our first calling as believers and what steps can we take to embrace that calling? (Our First Calling)

8. How can time dampen our zeal to commune with the Lord? How can the Spirit use time to increase our communion with the Lord? (Our First Calling)

9. If the disciples already understood the gospel message, why did Jesus send them to wait until the day of Pentecost to proclaim it? What can we learn from this in our own ministries? (A Spiritual Revival)

10. Why must God be the one who fans the flame of our hearts? What can we do to respond to his promises? (A Spiritual Revival)

NOTES

Chapter 1: A Tale of Two Departures

1. Jeffrey M. Jones, "U.S. Church Membership Falls below Majority for First Time," Gallup, March 29, 2021, https://news.gallup.com/poll/341963/church-membership-falls-below-majority-first-time.aspx.
2. "Church Attendance of Americans 2021," Statista, January 24, 2022, https://www.statista.com/statistics/245491/church-attendance-of-americans/.
3. The Fuller Institute, George Barna, and Pastoral Care Inc., "Why Pastors Leave the Ministry," Shepherds Watchmen, accessed March 1, 2022, https://shepherdswatchmen.com/browse-all-posts/why-pastors-leave-the-ministry/.

Chapter 2: The Heart of Ministry

1. Andrew Murray, *Humility: The Journey toward Holiness*, rev. ed. (New York: 1884; repr., Minneapolis: Bethany House, 2001), 17.

Chapter 3: Through Many Dangers, Toils, and Snares

1. *Autobiography of George Müller: Or a Million and a Half in Answer to Prayer,* comp. G. Fred Bergin (London: Pickering and Inglis, 1929), 152.

Chapter 4: Not Ashamed of the Gospel

1. Paul Purpura, "At Angola Prison, Short Timers Learn Trades, Coping Skills from Lifers," *Times-Picayune*, November 26, 2014, https://www.nola.com/news/crime_police/article_fe6d2fe0-876b-5bab-97a8-b9df194693d9.html.

2. *Miracle of Hope: The Brooklyn Tabernacle Singers at the Louisiana State Penitentiary* (The Brooklyn Tabernacle, 2008), DVD.

3. "Impact of Seminaries for Maximum Security Prisoners Will be Studied by Baylor University's Institute for Studies of Religion," Baylor University, October 9, 2012, https://www.baylor.edu/mediacommunications/news.php?action=story&story=123888.

4. "51% of Churchgoers Don't Know of the Great Commission," Barna, March 27, 2018, https://www.barna.com/research/half-churchgoers-not-heard-great-commission/.

5. *Samuel Chadwick*, ed. Norman G. Dunning (London: Hodder and Stoughton, 1933), 205.

Chapter 5: The Unabridged Bible

1. *Samuel Chadwick*, ed. Norman G. Dunning (London: Hodder and Stoughton, 1933), 207.

Chapter 6: Who's In Charge Here?

1. Paraphrase of John Owen, cited in Horatius Bonar, comp., *Words Old and New* (London: Nisbet, 1866), 196.

2. Samuel Chadwick, *The Way to Pentecost* (Berne, IN: Light and Hope, 1937), 7.

3. Edward Dennett, *His Victorious Indwelling*, ed. Nick Harrison (Grand Rapids: Zondervan, 1998), 343.

4. "Spirit of the Living God," by Daniel Iverson, copyright © 1935 Birdwing Music (ASCAP) (adm. at CapitolCMGPublishing.com) All rights reserved. Used by permission.

Chapter 7: Preaching in the Power of the Spirit

1. J. I. Brice, *The Crowd for Christ* (London: Hodder and Stoughton, 1934), 113.

2. "A Promise for Us and for Our Children," sermon no. 564, April 10, 1864, *365 Days with Spurgeon, Vol. 2: A Unique Collection of 365 Daily Readings from Sermons Preached by Charles Haddon Spurgeon from His Metropolitan Tabernacle Pulpit* (365 Days With Series), ed. Terence Peter Crosby (Day One Publications, 2002).

3. David Smithers, ed., *The Old Paths Magazine* 7 (August 2007), 14, https://archive.org/details/SID26164/page/n13/mode/2up.

Chapter 8: Unconditional Surrender

1. Wikipedia, s.v. "Yazidis," last edited February 15, 2022, 17:41, https://en.wikipedia.org/wiki/Yazidis#By_the_Islamic_State_of_Iraq_and_the_Levant_(ISIL).

2. Wilbur Chapman in Helen K. Hosier, *William and Catherine Booth: Founders of the Salvation Army*, Heroes of the Faith series (Uhrichsville, OH: Barbour, 1999), 202.

Chapter 9: Keep Watch

1. Letter from John Wesley to Molly Wesley, October 23, 1759, in *The Critic: A Literary Weekly, Critical and Eclectic, Volume 3 (January–June 1885)* (New York: Critic, 1885), 307.

2. David Roach, "Bible Reading Drops during Social Distancing," *Christianity Today*, July 22, 2020, https://www.christianitytoday.com/news/2020/july/state-of-bible-reading-coronavirus-barna-abs.html.

Chapter 10: Division Is Deadly

1. *The Collected Works of Abraham Lincoln*, ed. Roy Basler, Marion Dolores Pratt, and Lloyd A. Dunlap, vol. 2 (New Brunswick, NJ: Rutgers University Press, 2008), 491.

2. Bob Smietana, "Pastors Face a Growing Health Crisis," Lifeway Research, May 24, 2018, https://research.lifeway.com/2018/05/24/many-pastors-face-a-health-crisis-a-few-simple-tips-can-help/.

Chapter 11: Money

1. *Andrew A. Bonar: Diary and Letters*, ed. Marjory Bonar (London: Hodder and Stoughton, 1894), 349.
2. Ed Stetzer, "Bivocational Ministry as an Evangelism Opportunity," Wheaton College Billy Graham Center, November 2, 2017, https://wheatonbillygraham.com/bivocational-ministry-as-an-evangelism-opportunity/.